PRAISE FOR . . .

WINNING TOGETHER

"I have attended many workshops and read several books related to conflict resolution. WINNING TOGETHER is the approach that makes the most sense to me. This is an easy-to-follow step-by-step process to help resolve conflicts."
Parent of teenagers

"The WINNING TOGETHER approach helped me to develop a richer relationship with my children and bring harmony into my home."
Parent of preschool children

"WINNING TOGETHER gave me some great tools to help me resolve conflicts with my kids."
Parent of children aged 6 - 12

"WINNING TOGETHER gave me practical step-by-step solutions for resolving conflicts with my teenagers."
Parent of teenagers

"WINNING TOGETHER helped me to create a home where we achieved better respect for each other."
Parent of children aged 4 - 8

"WINNING TOGETHER showed me how to resolve conflicts with my kids while building their self-esteem."
Parent of children aged 6 - 9

(continued on the next page)

"WINNING TOGETHER helped me to restore some unity within our family."

Parent of teenagers

"WINNING TOGETHER helped me to stop and think about how to manage our family in a more positive way."

Parent of children aged 5 - 9

"WINNING TOGETHER helped me to better understand my children and be a better listener."

Parent of children aged 7 - 12

"WINNING TOGETHER helped me to be a better person and parent. It helped me to understand a process to achieve win-win solutions with my kids."

Parent of children aged 6 - 11

"WINNING TOGETHER helped me in a very positive way to think differently about my children."

Parent of children aged 8 - 11

"WINNING TOGETHER helped me to reduce the conflicts in our home and helped me to teach my kids anger management skills."

Parent of children aged 4 - 8

'WINNING TOGETHER showed me how to step back from a conflict and handle it in a way that reduces stress while creating lasting solutions. I have learned how to be calmer and more empathetic."

Parent of children aged 2 - 7

ALSO BY BRIAN HARRIS, B.A., M.Ed.

471 Timesavers For Busy People

Counseling For Teachers

Discovery

Explorations

The Joy of Teaching

Rainbows

Scholarship

The Self-Awareness Workbooks
(Volumes One + Two)

The Self-Esteem Books
(Volumes One + Two)

CGS COMMUNICATIONS, INC.

WINNING TOGETHER

SUCCESSFULLY RESOLVING CONFLICTS WITH YOUR KIDS

Brian Harris, B.A., M.Ed.

CGS Communications, Inc.
2521 Nicklaus Court
Burlington ON L7M 4V1
Canada

ISBN # 0-929079-30-2

Printed in Canada

10 9 8 7 6 5 4 3 2 1

For Steve, Tom, Sherina, and Caliesha

CONTENTS

PART TWO - RESOLVING CONFLICTS

PREFACE

It was a cold winter storm on an evening when spring should have been emerging. Forecasters had been warning for the past twenty-four hours that there would be a heavy snowfall, even though we were now in late March. During the day, the weather seemed to alternate between a blustery snow and freezing rain, leaving me in a quandary about an evening speaking engagement at the auditorium of a local hockey arena. Throughout the day, I expected my presentation on WINNING TOGETHER to be cancelled.

As the supper hour approached, and I had not heard from the organizers, I assumed that I was on as scheduled although it certainly appeared that the weather would discourage people from attending.

Arriving an hour before I was to speak, I was surprised to find some people already seated in the large auditorium. Little time passed before the seats were filled. It was soon clear that some audience members were going to have to stand. I was amazed at the turnout and further impressed by the enthusiasm and interest of those who attended on such a stormy evening.

It was apparent to me from the effort people made to attend this presentation on WINNING TOGETHER that there was a real need for parents (and teachers and other youth workers) to have practical proven tips on how to resolve conflicts with kids.

In the days that followed, I began to write my thoughts on WINNING TOGETHER as a possible book. A few more speaking engagements convinced me that there was a significant number of parents who wanted further assistance in understanding how to successfully resolve conflicts with their children.

Throughout this past year, I have received strong praise from people from all walks of life regarding WIN-NING TOGETHER. This book is an attempt to provide a more in-depth look at successfully resolving conflicts than I can generally present in the limited timeframes of half-day or evening workshops. It is the result of the many questions and comments people who have attended my seminars have presented to me. It is also the result of more than thirty years as an educator and counselor working in a multitude of educational environments.

WINNING TOGETHER is not just about resolving conflicts. It is also about teaching kids a process to help them learn lifelong skills in developing more positive relationships with others.

To each reader of this book, it is my sincere hope that WINNING TOGETHER will give you some ideas that will improve the quality of your relationship with your children.

INTRODUCTION

WINNING TOGETHER can help you to successfully resolve conflicts with your kids. WINNING TOGETHER can help to eliminate the stress, frustration, anger and sometimes even the violence that may accompany conflicts. WINNING TOGETHER can help your children become more responsible, more understanding, more respectful, and more likely to be successful in all areas of their lives.

Conflict is a natural, although generally unwelcome, part of living. The manner in which a conflict is handled can either escalate the problem or diffuse it. WINNING TOGETHER can help you to not only diffuse conflicts, but create win-win solutions that prevent further problems. In addition, WINNING TOGETHER can help you go one step further by turning conflicts into opportunities to teach your children lifelong skills in how to successfully resolve conflicts in their future.

We live in a rapidly changing world. Most people view change as a form of conflict. Conflict is generally viewed as a stressful event — something to be avoided. WINNING TOGETHER can help your kids learn to handle change and conflict in a positive manner. This can be invaluable to both their future happiness and success.

The conflicts your kids face in the home, in the community and at school can have a dramatic effect on how they feel about themselves. The self-esteem a child develops not only affects his/her present, but his/her hopes,

INTRODUCTION

dreams, ambitions, confidence level, success, and happiness as an adult as well.

It is no secret that kids are being exposed to more and more conflict situations. Research studies tell us that almost one-third of students are involved in bullying, either as a perpetrator or victim, at school. Similar studies tell us that more than one-third of students feel unsafe at school. Suicide amongst young people is a serious problem. Drugs and alcohol are readily available for the youngest of children. More than ever, kids need guidance from the adults who are a part of their lives. WINNING TOGETHER is a process that you can teach to your kids to help them better deal with these problems.

As you demonstrate effective conflict resolution skills, as taught to you in this book, your children can begin to learn these same skills through the example you show them.

Parenting is often a difficult job. Although parenting can bring satisfaction and happiness, it can also cause anguish and stress. WINNING TOGETHER provides you with practical ideas to help make you a more effective parent.

Ask yourself the following questions:

√ Do I sometimes get angry at my kids?

√ Are there times when I just want to give up?

√ Do I sometimes ignore conflicts with my kids?

INTRODUCTION

    √   Are there times when I just don't know how to respond to conflicts with my children?

    √   Are there situations with my kids when I lose my temper?

    √   Do my children sometimes make me cry?

    √   Are there times when my kids lose their temper with me?

    √   Do my kids make me feel exhausted?

    √   Do minor conflicts in our house turn into major battles?

    √   Do my children resist following much of what I say to them?

    √   Are my kids sometimes out of control?

If you found yourself answering YES to some of the above questions, then WINNING TOGETHER is a must-read for you. It is a book that can make a positive difference in your life.

By implementing the principles presented in this book, you can improve your relationship with your kids. You can also improve the way you feel about yourself as

INTRODUCTION

a parent. Best of all, as you implement WINNING TO-GETHER strategies, you will be helping your children to become responsible, respectful, and successful adults. Instead of viewing conflicts as roadblocks, you will begin to understand that conflicts can present opportunities for both you and your kids to strengthen your love for each other.

WINNING TOGETHER is an easy-to-read practical guide to help you successfully resolve conflicts with your children. The information is clear and concise. Case examples involving kids are provided with each step. Solutions are based on real life situations.

The content within WINNING TOGETHER is based on my experiences in working with literally thousands of kids of all ages. The questions answered are those presented to me by parents, teachers, counselors, social workers, and police officers who work with young people. The case studies presented are based on compilations of real life situations.

WINNING TOGETHER is divided into two parts. In PART ONE you will learn how to prevent some conflicts from occurring. In PART TWO you will learn the steps involved in resolving conflicts when they do occur.

Read on, and enjoy WINNING TOGETHER!

PART ONE

PREVENTING CONFLICTS

The easiest conflicts to resolve
are the ones that never happen.

PREVENTING CONFLICTS

INTRODUCTION

The first part of WINNING TOGETHER focuses on preventing or reducing conflicts in your home by helping you to establish a more positive relationship with your children.

Constantly handling conflicts with your kids can be frustrating, tiring, and time-consuming. When you prevent conflicts, you reduce the amount of stress in your home. You also give yourself more time. This time can be used to enjoy positive experiences with your children. It can also be used to effectively resolve the more serious conflicts you may encounter with your kids in a WINNING TOGETHER manner.

In PART ONE of WINNING TOGETHER, there are ten areas for you to consider which can help you to reduce or even prevent conflicts from occurring in your home. Not only can these strategies help you reduce the number of conflicts with your kids, they can also prevent more serious problems from happening.

The ideas presented in this book can also help you to develop mutual respect and rapport with your children.

PREVENTING CONFLICTS

By establishing a stronger relationship with your children, you will be building trust and cooperation. These ingredients can be helpful to you in successfully resolving more serious conflicts with your kids, if and when they do occur.

In many ways, the material presented in the first part of WINNING TOGETHER can help your kids feel more secure and accepted in your home. These two factors can make a significant impact on enhancing the self-esteem of your children.

In the next ten chapters, many ideas and concepts are presented. Most parents will find it useful to read the entire section of Part One first before returning to individual chapters to consider specific ideas to implement with their kids.

If you try to introduce too many strategies at once, you will likely meet with confusion and failure. Select those ideas you think will work best for you and introduce them one at a time. Effective parenting requires patience. As you consider any techniques discussed in this book, remember that one purposeful step carefully mastered can eventually help you scale the highest mountain.

PREVENTING CONFLICTS

The following are the ten chapter titles in PART ONE of WINNING TOGETHER:

1. PLAY WITH YOUR KIDS

2. BE INTERESTED IN YOUR KIDS

3. EMPHASIZE THE POSITIVE

4. LET SCHOOL HELP YOU

5. LISTEN MORE THAN YOU TALK

6. NO MEANS NO

7. TEACH TIME MANAGEMENT

8. PAY ATTENTION TO WHAT WORKS

9. WORK TOGETHER

10. BE A FRIEND TO YOURSELF

Taking some time to diminish the number of conflicts in your home can reduce stress, anger, arguments, and prevent more serious conflicts.

CHAPTER ONE

Play With Your Kids

When a parent gives a child his/her undivided attention, the child feels accepted, valued, and loved contributing to the healthy development of the child's self-esteem. Kids with strong self-esteem are more responsible, respectful and generally more successful throughout life.

Playing with your children is a wonderful way to give your kids attention. Playing together also creates a bond between you and your child, not to mention a time of fun and relaxation for all involved.

> Mike was ten years old when his parents divorced. He had close and regular contact with both parents. Although he maintained a good relationship with his father, he seemed to be constantly fighting with his mother. There was ongoing conflict and tension between them.
>
> In a counseling session, Mike expressed his concern that his mother never had time for him. "She is always talking on the telephone, watching TV, or reading a book." Mike's mother said she felt uncomfortable doing the things her son liked such as playing football or video games.
>
> One thing Mike's mother enjoyed was playing cards. A recommendation to teach her son some card games soon gave them something to do together. Once this occurred, Mike's anger towards her was greatly reduced.

PREVENTING CONFLICTS

Kids of varying ages have different needs related to playing with their parents. Young children may require far more time playing with their parents than a nineteen-year-old, although even the older teenager can benefit from engaging in some form of recreational activity with a parent.

Before considering a list of possible things that you can do with your children, there are a few rules of thumb.

Although kids benefit from playing with you, it is important to remember that they also need to play with their peers. Spending too much time playing with a parent can prevent a child from learning how to communicate and interact with other children.

Secondly, if your kids are involved in community activities (such as sports, dance, music, etc.), remember they still need time to play by themselves, with their peers, and with you. Some children, even at young ages, are on the go seven nights a week participating in community activities. Children need a healthy balance between structured activities, informal play, and sleep.

Thirdly, some kids, especially teenagers, may resist playing with you even though this time together could strengthen your relationship. While younger children may want some play time with you every day, your teenagers may feel more comfortable with something less frequent. You will find some ideas in the list beginning on page 25 that are more appropriate for teenagers (although many tips in this list are useful with children of all ages).

"Play With Your Kids"

Finally, as with other suggestions in this book, playing with your kids enhances your relationship with them when it is motivated by love.

In order for children to be loving, they must first feel loved!

PLAYING TOGETHER - SOME SUGGESTIONS

1. Once a week, set aside an hour or two for playing a favorite game. Take turns each week selecting the game (and like most of the other activities that follow, turn off the television).

2. Let your kids teach you something they learned at school and you, in turn, teach them something you learned at work.

PREVENTING CONFLICTS

3. Once in a while, go out for dessert.

4. Build something together using playdough, building blocks, etc.

5. Once a month, go to a show together. Take turns choosing the movie. After the film, go somewhere for a snack and discuss the film. All comments made must be positive.

6. Work on a jigsaw puzzle or crossword puzzle together.

7. Once a month, have a video night with your kids. Set themes for the evening with each person selecting a video appropriate to the theme.

8. Pick up vacation brochures at a travel agency and plan a dream trip together (this can be simply kept at a fantasy level or it may be a long term goal to actually take the trip together).

9. Exercise together.

10. Take an evening course together at a local community centre or college.

11. Go bowling, ice-skating, rollerblading, or horseback riding together.

12. Go out for dinner together (or breakfast, or lunch).

13. Go white-water rafting, on a canoe trip, or hiking together.

14. Enter a contest together.

"Play With Your Kids"

15. Read together. Exchange books. Exchange magazine articles.

16. Visit a country, a city, a museum or an art gallery together on the Internet.

17. Bake an exotic meal or dessert together.

18. Set aside one hour each week when you listen to each other's choice of music, alternating the choice every other week.

19. Invent a new game together.

20. Create a family painting with each member contributing to the final result.

21. Research your family heritage together.

22. Exchange roles for a night. Your kids become the parents and you become the kids.

23. Design and plant a garden together.

24. Make and fly kites together.

25. Use a video camera to film a movie that you create together.

and so on . . .

Understanding your child's world helps you to better understand your child.

CHAPTER TWO
Be Interested In Your Kids

It is not unusual to hear a parent, who is having some difficulties with a child, say, "I just don't understand him."

Taking the time to enter the world your kids experience can help you to understand the hopes, fears, successes, and failures they face daily. It also helps to establish a relationship that encourages them to talk to you

Jennifer, a fifteen-year old, became unbearable at home. She was angry, defiant and moody.   When she wasn't hiding in her room, she verbally attacked anyone who came near her. Jennifer's parents were at a loss to understand her behavior. The conflicts seemed to continue unabated.

The previous week, Jennifer stayed overnight at a friend's house. What she never told her parents was that her friend's parents weren't going to be home. She also avoided telling her parents that there would be boys, alcohol and drugs. She certainly didn't tell them that she ended up in bed with a guy.

Now, she was terrified she might be pregnant, or have some sexually transmitted disease, maybe even AIDS.

Jennifer was very angry at her parents. They had rarely insisted on curfews. They never verified her stories when she said she was going to be staying overnight at a friend's house. She blamed her parents for her possible predicament because they had never set any guidelines for her.

PREVENTING CONFLICTS

when they face problems.

Kids benefit from living in an environment with boundaries and standards. A sense of security results when you set expectations and take an interest in the lives of your children (more discussion will follow in Chapter Six regarding expectations). This chapter focuses on taking the time to enter your child's world. When children realize you are genuinely interested in all facets of their lives, they are less likely to be involved in serious conflicts.

Most parents would likely agree that it is easier to take an interest in a younger child than an older one. Some teenagers, and some youth even before this age, express resentment when parents question where they are going and who they are going to be with. Regardless of the reaction from older children and teenagers, it is nonetheless important to ask these questions. Although your kids may express anger at your apparent intrusion into their lives, your concern will be a practical demonstration of your love for them. Dealing with their reluctance to answer your questions is more desirable than dealing with the potential consequences of turning your kids loose to do whatever they want. Parents, who find themselves in such conflicts, should note that later chapters in this book will provide a framework for handling these conflicts with your kids in a positive manner.

Showing an interest in what your kids are doing at school is another way to let them know that you care about them.

"Be Interested In Your Kids"

At the beginning of the school year, or term, it would be useful to copy your child's timetable and a calendar (which most schools publish) of all the events, holidays, etc., that will be occurring during the school year. You are far more likely to get a response from a teenager when you ask a specific question about school, rather than the vague, "Well how was school today?" Having a copy of the timetable and calendar of events provides details of what is happening each day in your child's life, thus making it easier to ask specific questions.

For those parents who find themselves engaged in major conflicts by asking such questions, please be reassured there will be material later in this book to help you resolve these conflicts in a positive manner.

Some of the questions that kids have frequently suggested to me regarding what they think their parents should know about them are:

WHAT KIDS THINK THEIR PARENTS SHOULD KNOW ABOUT THEM

1. What subjects did I have today at school?

2. What are the names of all my teachers and what subjects do each of them teach?

3. What subject(s) at school do I find the most difficult?

4. What subject(s) do I excel in?

PREVENTING CONFLICTS

5. Who is my favorite teacher?

6. What is my favorite color?

7. What is my favorite television show?

8. What is my favorite book?

9. Who are my best two friends?

10. Where do my best two friends live, and do you have their phone numbers listed somewhere?

11. What is one of my biggest fears?

12. What is a dream that I have for my future?

13. What is my favorite song?

14. Who is my hero?

15. What makes me laugh?

16. When I'm not feeling so great, what is the easiest way to cheer me up?

17. Who are some of the people who have had a positive influence on my life?

18. What makes me feel good about myself?

19. Do I tend to be an optimist or a pessimist?

20. What is my strongest interest?

"Be Interested In Your Kids"

Well, how did you do? I will avoid attempting to provide an evaluation of your score. Every family and every situation is different. The intent of these questions is for you to think a little more about your involvement with your kids. It is possible to spend hours with your children on a regular basis and still not know them.

As you attempt to find out more about the life your child lives each day, it is important to remember your child will be more likely to let you into his life when you accept what he tells you without judging his comments. When kids feel a parent is going to find some fault with something they say, they are far more likely to avoid being open.

Listening without judging helps to create trust.

Catch your
kids
behaving
the way
you want
them to.

CHAPTER THREE
Emphasize The Positive

It is a lot easier to reward your kids for behaving the way you expect them to than it is to discipline them for inappropriate behavior.

Two siblings are screaming "bloody murder". A parent rushes into the room yelling for them to stop. A conflict quickly ensues regarding who is right or wrong. Such situations are often stressful. Unfortunately, resolutions are often temporary, sometimes lasting only a matter of minutes before the next conflict develops.

Let's look at another scenario. Two siblings are actually playing well together. A parent enters the room and rewards their positive behavior. The parent tells them it is terrific that they are able to decide on a fair way of playing without having to yell or scream at each other. Another time, in a similar situation, the parent enters the room and simply watches the kids play. The children are learning that they can receive a parent's attention without having to misbehave. They are also learning that they are capable of resolving many day-to-day conflicts on their own without requiring help from their parents.

A large part of emphasizing the positive relates to the use of praise. Praise is a powerful way to prevent conflicts in your home. When you reinforce the behavior that you want from your kids, there is a good chance they will repeat that behavior again. The more they repeat appropriate behavior, the more this behavior is likely to become a positive habit.

PREVENTING CONFLICTS

In using praise, there a few guidelines to remember that will help make the praise more effective. The most powerful forms of praise are specific. For example, your child brings home his report card. A general statement from you such as, "Good boy," is not as strong as specific statements such as, "Look what your teacher wrote about your work in science. She says your work is always done on time, you participate well in class and your test results are excellent." Specific praise, such as this, helps to maintain specific behavior like continuing to have work done on time, participating well in class and achieving excellent test results.

Your daughter plays on a local baseball team. After a game, you praise her profusely for hitting a home run. The next game, there are no home runs and your praise is simply, "Good game." Repeat this same pattern over ten or fifteen games and your daughter is likely to begin to think that the only thing that really matters in playing baseball is hitting home runs. If she reaches the point where she rarely hits home runs anymore, she may very well lose her interest in playing baseball.

Looking at this same situation in another way, you praise your daughter after a game for listening to the coach's instructions, or running down a ground ball, or congratulating another player on a good play, or keeping a positive attitude after striking out, or correctly thinking about where the ball should be thrown after catching it, and on the list could go. With these types of specific praise, enjoying the game and feeling good about playing it no longer depend on just hitting home runs.

Specific praise helps to create specific habits.

Kids need to receive attention from their parents. As hard as it is to understand, most kids would rather be yelled at by their parents than be ignored. In such instances, they may misbehave simply to receive attention from their parents. In these situations, a child may continue to exhibit the undesirable behavior long after the parent finally realizes that yelling and even punishments are not stopping the problem.

Habits can be hard to change, generally requiring patience and a concerted effort. This is a fantastic reason for reinforcing positive behavior when your kids demon-

PREVENTING CONFLICTS

strate it.

When Tanya was a young child, her parents were extremely busy attempting to meet financial obligations. Tanya spent a great deal of time in daycare centers and with babysitters. Even when her parents were at home, they rarely had much time for their daughter.

Over time, Tanya learned that temper tantrums were a good way to get attention from her parents. Although the tantrums resulted in strong words and sometimes discipline from her parents, Tanya still craved the attention. By the time her parents realized the tantrums were increasing in quantity and intensity, Tanya had developed a habit that took on a life of its own.

Her parents found themselves facing major conflicts with their daughter every day of the week and sometimes more than once on the same day. They tried a calmer approach to her tantrums with little effect. They tried rewarding good behavior, but the tantrums continued. Regardless of their approach, Tanya seemed to find some excuse to display her temper. Tanya's habit continued long after the initial reasons that caused it disappeared.

Eventually, with the help of a counselor, the parents were able to reduce the number of tantrums by maintaining a consistent approach over many months. The approach included repetitive low key responses to her tantrums and a systematic effort to specifically praise appropriate behavior whenever it occurred.

"Emphasize The Positive"

Most adults realize how difficult it is to change a habit. Unfortunately, when we think of habits, we often associate the word "bad" more than "good". Habits, though, can be positive. This realization is integral to understanding the importance of giving your kids specific praise. Specific praise can help your kids learn good habits. What parent wouldn't want a son or daughter who does his/her homework without being told to do it, or does chores around the house without being reminded, or keeps his/her room clean without being nagged? When kids consistently behave in a positive manner without our need to tell them what to do, they have likely developed positive habits.

A key component of this chapter relates to the importance of catching your kids doing what you want them to do. It is often easier for your kids to attract your attention when they scream, fight or refuse to do what you have asked them. It may require more diligence for you to give them attention when they are playing appropriately with their siblings, or when they are completing their homework, or tidying their rooms.

Give some thought to the traits you want your children to possess as adults. If you want your kids to be responsible, give your strongest and most specific praise for things they do that demonstrate a sense of responsibility. If you think initiative would be an important trait for your kids to possess, then give your kids specific praise when you catch them showing initiative.

PREVENTING CONFLICTS

*Good habits
are the
building blocks
of future
success.*

Praising your children does not mean that you ignore inappropriate behavior. Kids can benefit from constructive criticism and guidance when this is necessary. The final part of this book will give you a framework for resolving conflicts that you can use to help your kids grow in positive ways even when they are engaged in conflicts with you.

Finally, praise should not be a buffer to deliver criticism. Most adults can relate to being given some form of praise at work only to receive some form of criticism in the next sentence. In such situations, there is a tendency to remember the criticism more than the praise. If you have to combine praise and criticism, it makes more sense to start with the criticism and end with the praise, putting greater attention on the praise. When it is necessary to simply give constructive criticism, then do it without feeling the need to mix it with praise.

Some parents may find praise ineffective with their children. In such situations, it is useful to take a closer look at how praise is being given. For example, quality of praise is far more important than quantity. Most readers can likely think of someone who praises every little thing that happens, often out of habit. For these people, their praise is often ineffective, sometimes even causing an adverse reaction. Praise should only be given when it is deserved. Kids appreciate specific praise when they have done something to earn it. On the other hand, some kids will find undeserved praise offensive and may even rebel against it by misbehaving. In addition, praise should always be sincere. Sarcasm and insincerity can undermine the effectiveness of any praise.

Finally, in emphasizing the positive, an eventual goal should be to help your kids internalize praise. Instead of sentences such as, "I am very proud of you," you might use a response such as, "You must feel very proud of yourself." Kids will be happier and more successful when they learn to reward themselves for positive accomplishments. Strong self-esteem accompanies kids who don't have to always depend on others to feel good about themselves.

School
can be
your
best friend.

CHAPTER FOUR
Let School Help You

In simple terms, school has a huge effect on your child's self-esteem. In turn, self-esteem has a major impact on the number of conflicts that you encounter with your child.

There are many facets of school that could be considered as you attempt to reduce or eliminate various conflicts in your home. I will look at the five questions that parents most often ask me. These questions are:

1. How can I help my child to be more successful at school?

2. How can I get my child to do his/her homework?

3. What can I do if my child dislikes school?

4. What can I do if my child is being bullied?

5. What can I do if my child works hard, but achieves poor results?

PREVENTING CONFLICTS

*Success
at school
can make a huge
difference
in what happens
at home.*

A brief discussion of each of these five questions is as follows:

1. HOW CAN I HELP MY CHILD TO BE MORE SUCCESSFUL AT SCHOOL?

Although there are many possible answers to this question, including helping to develop a positive attitude, good work habits and communicating effectively, I believe, based on working with thousands of kids of all ages, the single factor that affects success at school for most children relates to reading. While some kids can definitely overcome reading difficulties to find success, most of them gain either confidence or suffer frustration at school as a result of their reading ability. A child can have superior ability in mathematics, only to have her work affected in a detrimental way by failing to understand the wording of problems. Similarly, most other subjects demand a level of reading ability in order to be successful. Yes, there are exceptions and yes, some kids compensate. My answer is based on helping most kids and not the exceptions to the rule.

I believe most kids would benefit at school from a home that encourages a love for reading. For those parents who have younger children, taking the time to read to them, and not just when they are going to bed, can be very helpful. Reading should be fun. Take your kids to the library often. Help your kids by shutting off the television and having a family reading hour. Talk about what you read. Set an example by reading yourself and telling your kids what you learn as you read.

When kids read with good fluency, speed and solid comprehension, they have a tremendous advantage in achieving success at school and beyond.

Unfortunately, some parents may find, in spite of great encouragement, that their child encounters difficulties in reading, perhaps as the result of some learning problem. While some kids with poor reading skills compensate with terrific verbal skills or some other talents/strengths, others suffer low self-esteem as the result of struggling with their inability to read.

You can help your kids rebuild their self-esteem by

helping them to understand and appreciate their other strengths. Focus on their strengths while you continue the best you can do to provide remedial assistance for their weaknesses.

Strengths can be the building blocks for developing strong self-esteem.

Consult with your child's teachers and the staff at educational supply stores for the names of games, puzzles, books, DVD's, software, etc., that might help your child improve his or her reading skills. Emphasize reading in a manner that appeals to your child.

"Let School Help You"

As a young boy, Mark was happy and enjoyed school. His marks were average although his teachers often commented on his excellent attitude and good work habits. Mark's only weakness in his early school years related to his slowness in reading.

As Mark approached the middle school years, he maintained average success through hard work. Although he spent hours each night completing his homework, he was determined to do well. His teachers often commented in a positive way on his good attitude.

In junior high school, Mark began to experience some problems at school. He was frustrated by his inability to keep pace with other kids. He understood the work, but never seemed to have enough time to finish his assignments. He studied hard for tests, and thought he understood the material, but his results were generally worse than he anticipated. Slowly, his attitude at home and at school began to change. It became easier for him to give up instead of working hour after hour just to keep pace with his peers.

By the time Mark reached senior high school, he no longer enjoyed school. His peer group changed. He began to experiment with drugs and alcohol. His relationship with both his parents and teachers was strained. He often missed school. When he did attend, he was a behavior problem in many of his classes.

In his first year of senior high school, Mark's results

PREVENTING CONFLICTS

were dismal. It was only after a teacher suggested that Mark enter a cooperative education (work experience) program for his next semester that he agreed to return to school.

The work experience program was a tremendous success for Mark. He regained his sense of worth. His attitude changed as he began to feel better about himself.

After his work experience program, Mark returned back to school where his courses were carefully chosen to best match his interests and abilities. With success, Mark regained his good work habits. As school became an enjoyable place for him again, he quickly left a negative peer group and improved his relationship with both his parents and teachers.

After graduating from high school, Mark attended a local community college, building on his strengths. In spite of difficulties in reading, Mark found success in life.

2. HOW CAN I GET MY CHILD TO DO HIS/HER HOMEWORK?

One of the greatest sources of conflict for parents and kids often relates to homework. These conflicts often include concerns about television viewing, playing video games and/or telephone usage. While it may be easy to shut off a television to resolve this concern, it is not as easy to control what your kids are doing on a computer. While pretending to do homework, some kids may be playing games on their computers.

Some kids may even spend a significant amount of time doing homework with poor results because their approach is ineffective.

Like many other areas of success, completing homework in a meaningful manner is a habit that is learned. There are a number of things you can do to help your kids develop routines that will help form such a habit.

To ensure your kids are actually doing their homework, it is very helpful to know what it is that they have to complete each night. Encourage your kids to keep a record of homework assignments in each class during the day. A small calendar or daybook would suffice. Your son/daughter could use a computer to create a daily calendar that corresponds to each of his/her classes with spaces for homework assignments, upcoming tests and even the topics (including text reference page numbers) related to work done during today's classes. Give specific praise to your kids for keeping track of the homework that they are required to do each night.

For parents whose kids refuse to follow this basic step in organizing themselves, it may be necessary to discuss your concerns (focusing on what you are attempting to do) with their teachers. Some teachers will willingly ensure that your kids write down their assignments. Others may provide for you an outline of upcoming assignments, tests, etc., covering a week or a month period of time. And others may even list homework assignments on a school Website. When parents and teachers work

PREVENTING CONFLICTS

together, amazing things can be accomplished for kids.

One of your goals, related to homework, is helping your children form positive habits. Once these habits are in place, this will be one major area that you will no longer have to face constant conflicts with them. Routines are an important aspect of forming these habits. Ten tips that can help your kids develop successful homework habits are:

10 TIPS TO HELP YOUR KIDS DEVELOP POSITIVE HOMEWORK HABITS

1. Establish a regular time for doing homework. This should be earlier in the evening, rather than later. Consider turning off any televisions in the house during this time.

2. Your kids should prioritize what they have to do, always starting with their most difficult tasks.

3. Your children should establish a rough framework with timelines to be followed in completing each homework assignment.

4. In the beginning stages of forming these positive habits, check with your kids every once in a while to see if they are following the schedule and timetable that they have set for the evening.

"Let School Help You"

5. A small, and sometimes a major, part of the evening should be scheduled to work on any assignments, or study for any tests, that are due at some future time. Help your kids understand how doing a little each day can make a significant contribution to the final result.

6. Emphasize the importance of taking healthy breaks such as walks, exercise, fresh air, healthy snacks, etc.

7. As your children finish each item they listed on their initial schedule for the evening, they should cross it off with a bold line. This is a form of self-reward which helps your kids internalize their success instead of depending on you at each step for approval.

8.   When studying for tests, one of the most widely recommended techniques, that can help many kids learn effectively, is writing a summary of what they have just studied. In addition, it helps to write answers to possible questions that might be asked on the test. For some kids, stating summaries or answers to potential questions to you verbally might work better. Such children might also benefit from recording their answers to possible questions.

9. Encourage your kids to show you the work they complete each evening. In addition to praising the work that has been done, react positively to their attempts to follow the homework schedule that they established for the evening.

10. When your children work hard at completing their homework, but seem to lack understanding, it may be useful to consult with their teacher(s) concerning their ability level. Sometimes, you may have to arrange some form of tutoring to help your child to be successful.

PREVENTING CONFLICTS

3. WHAT CAN I DO IF MY CHILD DISLIKES SCHOOL?

When kids dislike school, there are generally three possible reasons. First, they might be frustrated by the level of work. Second, they might be victims of bullying (or be involved in some form of conflict with someone at school). Third, they might have no friends. A combination of two, or in the worst case all three, can certainly contribute to kids strongly disliking school.

The next two pages will take a look at questions 1 + 3. Bullying will be considered as a separate topic later in this chapter (see page 53).

When children are struggling with their schoolwork, or when they have failed to do their homework or prepare for tests, they sometimes feign an illness to stay home. Once this happens, there are a some negative results. First, they fall further behind at school due to their absence which often increases their anxiety about school. Second, they learn that an illness can be a technique for avoiding responsibility. If this pattern is repeated enough times, your kids may learn a bad habit which can be difficult to change. At the first sign of your children not wanting to go to school, listen to their concerns. If necessary, consult with their teachers. Attempt to resolve any concerns raised by either your kids or their teachers.

Sometimes, when kids struggle with their schoolwork, they become behavioral problems in the class. In such situations, conflicts can develop between your children and their teachers.

Whenever your child is suggesting he is having a

conflict with a teacher, make an appointment to see the teacher involved. Get all the facts. Where possible, work together with the teacher to resolve the issues. When you fail to resolve the concerns with the teacher, consult with the principal.

Finally, there are some kids who do not have any friends at school. These kids are not necessarily being bullied in the traditional sense of the word. Nevertheless, school can be a miserable place for such children. Your child's teacher may be able to help in such a situation. In many schools, kids can help as volunteers for younger children which often helps them feel more accepted. In some schools, younger children who may be encountering difficulties may be helped by an older student who is a peer helper. In both of these situations, kids can gain more confidence which often helps them to form new friendships. You can also assist your child in developing friendships with other kids by involving them in community activities.

4. WHAT CAN I DO IF MY CHILD IS BEING BULLIED?

School can be a terrible place if your child is being bullied. Various research studies show that 25-33% of students are targets of bullying. If your kids suddenly start to cry, dislike school, withdraw, and/or demonstrate unexpected anger outbursts (especially in playing with younger siblings, pets or toys), it may be possible that they are victims of bullying.

Unfortunately, many kids don't share their fears con-

PREVENTING CONFLICTS

cerning being bullied. It is important to talk to your child and watch for evidence if you suspect he/she is being bullied. Volunteering to drive your kids and their friends to or from school, or helping as a volunteer on a class field trip, may give you an opportunity to observe what is happening with your child.

Bullying should be immediately confronted. Ignoring it can make the problem worse.

> Suddenly, one day in class, Jeff, a normally quiet teenager, attacked William, another student, punching him repeatedly. In the ensuing investigation regarding the assault, it was found that Jeff had been a victim of bullying since the age of seven.
>
> When Jeff was seven, his father died causing him to retreat from other kids. Unfortunately, most kids didn't understand the reason for Jeff's change of behavior. Some kids began to taunt him. As students began to pick on him verbally, Jeff withdrew even more from his peers. As time went on, some kids even bullied him physically.
>
> By the time Jeff became a teenager, he no longer had any friends. He lived in constant fear of going to school. By this time, the bullying was both persistent and subtle.
>
> It was discovered that the student who Jeff attacked had been bullying him in one form or another for more than eight years.
>
> A counselor met with both Jeff and the student he had assaulted. In the discussions that followed, it turned out that William had constantly been bullied by one of his

"Let School Help You"

> parents over a period of years.
>
> As both boys began to understand each other better, they formed a token friendship out of respect for what each of them was going through. While they never became best friends, William did go out of his way at school to be considerate of Jeff. In the process, William set an example for other students to do the same. Soon, Jeff was able to form some friendships with others.

If you suspect your kids are being bullied, consult with their teachers. Many schools have bullying programs. Teachers can be an excellent resource in helping your kids to avoid being victims.

Most bullying victims are perceived by other students as being weaker in some way. Students rarely bully those who have strong self-esteem. Students also rarely bully others who have a strong group of friends unless the whole group is bullied which occasionally happens. To help bully-proof your kids, consider the following recommendations:

1. Involve your kids in community activities such as sports. Being a part of a team can build self-esteem and help your kids to assert themselves in positive ways. It can also build friendships and help your kids belong to positive peer groups.

2. Provide assertiveness training either through counseling or involvement in activities such as judo, karate, etc.

3. Show your kids how to be assertive with others.

PREVENTING CONFLICTS

4.   Ask yourself if you sometimes find yourself as a victim in your relationship with others (including your spouse/partner). Your kids often learn much of their behavior from the manner in which you react to others. If you are a victim or have trouble asserting yourself, you could help your kids (and yourself) by getting help.

5. Enroll your kids in a bully-proof program as offered in their school or in your community.

6. Role-play bullying situations at home to allow your kids to practice assertive responses.

7. Encourage your kids to talk about it.

8. Ask your child's teacher for help.

9. Help your kids develop friendships with others.

10. Success at school builds your child's self esteem and strong self-esteem helps to   prevent bullying.

*Children tend
to learn the most
by watching
what their parents do,
not what their
parents say.*

5. WHAT CAN I DO IF MY CHILD WORKS HARD, BUT ACHIEVES POOR RESULTS?

School can be an incredibly frustrating experience for a child who works hard, but achieves poor results. If your child has strong homework habits, yet seems to struggle to achieve average, or below-average results, it is possible there are other factors which may be preventing success. These factors may include poor reading skills, failure to account for unique learning styles, some form of learning disability, emotional and psychological concerns, unresolved family concerns, etc. Both teachers and sometimes even family doctors may be appropriate first steps in helping your child.

I believe the following questions are appropriate to ask your child's teachers:

1. What is my child's reading comprehension level?

2. What is my child's attitude at school?

3. What kinds of things seem to cause frustration for my child in class?

4. How does my child react to frustration at school?

5. What are my child's strengths and weaknesses?

6. How does my child interact with other students?

7. Does my child appear to be focused at school?

PREVENTING CONFLICTS

8.   Is the written work that my child does at a significantly different level than the verbal ability she demonstrates in class?

9. What can you do to help my child become more successful at school?

10. What can I do to help my child become more successful at school?

The following represent some questions you should ask yourself as a parent.

1. Have my child's eyes and ears (seeing and hearing) been tested recently?

2. Has my child been exposed to a family conflict that is unresolved for my child? If so, is my child receiving professional counseling?

3. When my child is doing schoolwork, are distractions such as loud music and/or television eliminated?

4. Is my child getting enough sleep each night?

5. Is my child eating healthy foods?

6. Does my child understand some basic strategies in time management? (There will be further discussion in this area in Chapter Seven.)

7. Would my child benefit from private tutoring?

8. Have I followed any recommendations made by my child's teacher?

9. Is the level of my child's program at school appropriate to his/her level of ability?

10. After considering all of the above questions, have I consulted with my family doctor?

> Cathy was an eight year old girl that seemed to be constantly sick. She often suffered from headaches and stomach pains. It was generally very difficult to get her to go to school even on days when she seemed to be well. Several appointments with a family doctor revealed no specific concerns.
>
> Cathy's teacher said that she was a hard-working student when she was at school, but experienced a great deal of frustration because she was constantly behind in her work due to her absences. She read slowly, but readily participated in discussions related to most topics studied in class.
>
> Although Cathy's parents often read to her at home, they never asked Cathy to read to them. One evening, the girl's mother asked her to read aloud. She was shocked at the difficulty her daughter exhibited in reading. The otherwise talkative girl, who seemed to understand when others read to her, read methodically with poor understanding.
>
> Eventually, Cathy was diagnosed as having a learning disability. With additional support at school and with teaching strategies that were appropriate to her disability, Cathy began to enjoy better success. With the success, her illnesses began to disappear and school became a more enjoyable place for her.

Effective
listening
is
the great
encourager.

CHAPTER FIVE
Listen More Than You Talk

One of the least understood and most difficult communication skills to master is listening. In my experience with kids of all ages, one of the single greatest complaints that many children have regarding their parents is, "They don't listen to me." And many parents would likely make the same statement regarding their kids. The good news is that as you improve your listening skills, you will be teaching your children how to improve their ability to listen to you as well. The comments that follow are in many ways an introduction to more specific listening skills that will be discussed in more detail in Part Two of WINNING TOGETHER when you begin to look at specific techniques for resolving conflicts.

As the title of this chapter suggests, one of the basic ways to improve your listening skills is to listen more than you talk. It is normal, especially in a conflict situation, to want to express your point of view. Effective listening requires patience (often in the form of biting one's tongue).

When children feel they are being listened to, many conflicts are avoided before they occur. Conflicts are often the result of both misunderstanding and pent-up emotions that have not had a chance to be expressed. When kids feel comfortable talking to their parents, they have the opportunity to express their concerns (whether they are school, peer, sibling, or parent related) before these concerns reach a conflict level.

PREVENTING CONFLICTS

Some parents tell me that they just can't get their kids to talk to them. The following three considerations may assist with this problem, although it is important to remember that listening more than you talk is a key component to the success of each of these.

1. AVAILABILITY

It is difficult for your children to talk to you when you are unavailable. When your kids need to converse with you, they want to feel that they have your undivided attention. If you are always busy, whether working or watching TV, it is difficult for them to find the right moment to talk. The longer this pattern is repeated, the less likely you are to have them communicate openly about what is happening to them at school or with their friends.

Be sensitive to opportunities for listening to what your kids have to tell you. When they begin to talk, don't hesitate to shut off the TV or stop working. Give them your complete attention. Let them know that you are interested in what they have to say. The more sincere you are in wanting to listen to them, the more sincere they will be in telling you what is on their mind.

Some parents find that there is a specific time which is the best moment for quality conversation. Recognize such moments and be conscious of repeating them. For example, most kids attempt to delay going to bed. This may be a perfect WINNING TOGETHER situation for your child and you. By sitting on the edge of your child's bed at this time, you give her an opportunity to delay going to sleep for a brief time while you engage in meaningful conversation. Not only does this provide a time for dialogue, it may also provide an appropriate way for your child to "slow down" before sleeping.

2. SPECIFIC QUESTIONS

Many parents find that questions such as, "How was school today?" often bring a shrug or a one word answer such as, "Okay." Chapter Two talked about the importance of taking an interest in your child's life. When you are aware of specific things that your child is involved in, it is easier to ask specific questions which often result in a more fluent conversation.

For example, instead of, "How was school today?" you might ask one of the following questions:

- tell me a little about the assembly on bullying you had today at school

- tell me some of the questions you had on your history test today

- tell me some of the things your classmates brought for "show and tell"

- tell me about the science experiment you were working on today

- tell me a little about what you did in gym class today

and so on . . .

3. ACCEPTANCE

Most people are more open to talking when they feel unconditionally accepted by the person they are talking to. If one of your goals is to have your kids talk more openly to you, it is important to respect them as they talk to you. This does not mean that you have to discard your standards or blindly accept something you are opposed to. Your careful listening can help your child to feel accepted.

By accepting your children, you are encouraging them to talk freely to you. This will help you to better understand their point of view and any concerns they may be facing. This often helps to prevent conflicts before they occur. By accepting your kids, you are also teaching them to show respect for you when it is time to present your point of view.

Acceptance is integral to the development of your child's self-esteem.

During those times when you disagree with what is being said, focus on restating (paraphrasing) what your kids are saying to you. This can pave the way for meaningful dialogue to help resolve possible conflicts (there is more specific information on paraphrasing in Chapter 13).

Acceptance can also be shown through eye-contact, body language, remaining calm, and by stopping whatever else you are doing to listen. Kids sense very quickly when an adult (especially a parent) is sincere. When a parent genuinely cares about a child, this underscores all communication in a very positive manner.

The ability
to say "NO"
convincingly
can become
a lifelong
asset
for your
kids.

CHAPTER SIX

No Means No

One of the single greatest causes of problems throughout life for many people is the inability to say "NO." Some people find themselves in unhealthy relationships because they are unable to say no to a dominant partner. Others are overworked because they are unable to say no to their boss and/or co-workers. Some people find themselves constantly battling troubling addictions because they are unable to say no to their temptations. And others find themselves as victims, sometimes because of an inability to stand up for themselves.

Kelly grew up in a home where "no" rarely meant "no". At an early age, she learned that no generally turned into a yes if she persisted in what she wanted. When it was time for bed, she quickly learned that she could stretch five more minutes into ten, and then fifteen, until by the time she was a teenager her parents had given up on trying to enforce any rules related to going to bed.

In her preschool years, she learned that temper tantrums or being cute could quickly dissolve the firmest no from her parents into a yes. When she was told to clean up her room or else, the "or else" always turned out to be one of her parents cleaning up her room for her. In her early teenage years when she was told to come home on time, or she would not be permitted to go out again the following night, she

> disregarded the rules, and still managed to convince her parents that things would be different if they let her go out again the next evening.
>
> Kelly grew up thinking that no really meant yes and that consequences for breaking any rules could be manipulated to her satisfaction. Unfortunately, at the age of thirteen, Kelly became involved in drugs and promiscuous sex. She had never learned to say no which made her an easy target. Never having faced consequences that were inconvenient to her for her behavior, she thought she was invincible.
>
> It took a serious drug problem and several pregnancies to bring Kelly and her parents to the stark realization that "no" can be one of the most powerful and positive words in anyone's vocabulary.

Kids need limits. They benefit in a positive way from having parents who set boundaries for their behavior. When kids disregard these boundaries without facing consequences, they learn to view life in an inappropriate way. People who disobey rules get into trouble. In my work with adults, I have often found that those who struggle to maintain either jobs or relationships are often people who lack a sense of personal responsibility and who have difficulty accepting rules or standards of appropriate behavior.

Although saying no to a child may initially cause some conflict in the home, in the long run it can help to prevent more serious problems. A child is told to stop coloring on a wall, or her crayons will be taken away. The child persists. Her crayons are taken away. She cries. The parent gives the crayons back to the child to stop the crying. The girl is beginning to learn that no does not necessarily mean no.

When you say no to your children you are not only helping to teach them appropriate behavior, you are teaching them that no means no. The manner in which your kids say no to others is often a reflection of how you say no to them. When your kids are offered illicit drugs, they may say no in the way that you say it to them. When your kids become adults, they may respond to unrealistic demands either from an employer, co-worker, or partner in the manner in which you taught them as you say no to their inappropriate behavior as children (and also in the manner in which you say no to unrealistic demands from your employer, co-workers, and spouse/partner).

No is a very powerful word. Unfortunately, many people view this word as negative. In reality, it is one of the most positive words in our vocabulary. Most adults reading this book can likely think of situations where your failure to reply to a situation with a convincing no caused personal pain and hardship.

It is sometimes difficult for parents to understand how a two-letter word like no can make such a significant impact on preventing future conflicts with their kids, especially when some kids have such an extreme reaction to the word. Some parents simply find it easier to give in to the tears, temper tantrums or persistence of a young child than to maintain their resolve. The earlier your kids learn that no means no, the sooner you will eliminate many of the conflicts that can continue to persist if you fail to be firm with them.

For parents reading this book who have difficulty saying no, it is recommended that you find additional reading materials in learning to be assertive (on page 71 are some tips to help you be more assertive). In some cases, it would be useful to discuss your concerns with a professional counselor. Kids learn best by what they see. The best way to teach your kids how to say no is by setting an example for them.

While some parents have difficulty saying no, there may be other readers whose difficulty lies in saying no aggressively and unrealistically. We live in a rapidly changing world. Kids who learn to understand different points of view and who are able to maintain a degree of flexibility in achieving their personal goals are more likely to achieve happiness and success in life than those who have rigid expectations of themselves and others. Although there are times when a parent needs to say no, there are other times when it is useful to consider your child's point of view and adapt a flexible approach to resolving conflicts (there will be further discussion on this in the second part of this book).

Some suggestions to help you be more assertive and effective in saying no are provided on the following page.

"No Means No"

<u>TIPS TO HELP YOU BE MORE ASSERTIVE</u>

1. Begin your sentences with "I" instead of "you". For example, you might say, "I feel angry when you . . ." instead of "You make me angry." The basic sentence structure to learn is, "I feel . . . when you . . ." or "When you . . . I feel . . . ."

2. If you are going to say no, say it right away. Be direct and keep your sentences short and to the point.

3. When you are not sure that you understand what has happened, ask questions to clarify before responding.

4. Remain calm and in control.

5. Use factual descriptions instead of judging your kids. For example, you might say, "Your clothes are scattered over the floor," instead of "You live like a pig."

6. Keep your voice firm and maintain eye contact.

7. Talk about specific behaviors and not your child's character. For example, you might say, "When you don't do your homework, I get upset," instead of "You're lazy."

8. If necessary, keep repeating your message, keeping it direct and simple.

9. Focus on the point you want to make.

10. Respect your kids and their point of view.

PREVENTING CONFLICTS

11. Be realistic when you state possible consequences. Avoid making empty threats. For example, you might say, "You can't watch TV until you have completed your homework," instead of "You are not allowed to watch TV for the next month." The first statement is far easier and more realistic for you to enforce than the second.

12. Eliminate your anger before you speak.

13. Choose the best time and place to talk to your child. It may be a losing battle for you to state your concerns when your child is with a friend (even if it is a sibling).

14. You have the right to say no without feeling guilty.

15. Practice saying no in situations that don't involve your kids.

16. Ignoring conflicts is one of the surest ways to encourage problems to get worse.

17. Be aware of the thoughts that are running through your mind. We all have a tendency to think the worst in a conflict situation. Replace your negative thinking with a positive picture of how you want a specific problem with your child to be resolved.

18. Avoid exaggerations. For example you might say, "This is the third time I have told you to get started on your homework," instead of "You never do your homework."

19. Be honest and direct about your feelings and needs.

"No Means No"

20. Avoid sarcasm and absolute statements such as, "You always . . . ."

21. You may find it more comfortable to say no if you stop and think of the possible consequences if you give in.

22. If you are going to say no, always be prepared to state your reason.

23. Seek win-win solutions instead of win-lose solutions.

24. Take some time to think things over before responding.

25. Ask yourself (or consult with someone whose opinion you respect) whether your expectations are reasonable.

26. Take action on what you have control over.

27. Keep things in perspective. It is important to remember that kids at different ages go through stages as part of their normal development. Attempt to understand the stages and work with your child in moving through the stages in a positive manner.

28. It is human nature to seek the easy way out. Always do what is right, not what is easy.

29. Focus on what you want your children to do instead of what you don't want them to do.

30. If you know someone who is an assertive parent, observe them carefully and imitate what they do.

When life
seems to be
passing you
by,
look for
a ramp
to take you
off the
highway.

CHAPTER SEVEN

Teach Time Management

One of the commonest complaints of most adults is that there just doesn't seem to be enough time in a day. This is often magnified for those who are parents. Conflicts sometimes occur in a home because time pressures leave family members feeling rushed which can contribute to misunderstanding when communication occurs.

Unfortunately, time is constant and can't be managed. The real solution to having more time for meaningful family interaction is found in self-management. Introducing techniques and strategies that can help all family members to better manage themselves will help to eliminate potential conflicts.

Five considerations to help both you and your kids to feel less rushed and stressed as a result of time concerns are:

1. **Focus on what is most important.**

2. **Plan each day before you begin.**

3. **Large tasks are just a series of small steps.**

4. **Never misplace something twice.**

5. **Listening is time well invested.**

1. FOCUS ON WHAT IS MOST IMPORTANT

At work, being busy and being productive are not necessarily the same thing. At home, being busy and being a WINNING TOGETHER parent are not necessarily the same thing either.

A basic question for every parent to ask is, "What is important for your children?" Based on the material presented so far in this book, there are strong arguments to be made for things such as taking time to play with your kids, ensuring your kids have sufficient opportunities to complete their schoolwork, and having time to listen to them. Your list of what is important could also include other things such as encouraging your children to be involved in your community, your church, sports, the arts, completing chores, etc.

Whatever you identified as being most important becomes your focus (and it is certainly useful to get feedback from your kids in identifying what is important to them). Anything that disrupts this focus needs to be addressed.

Once you have established your focus, become aware of any distractions that interrupt it. In most families, telephones, computers, video games and televisions are the biggest culprits. To maintain your focus, there may be times when you have to pull some plugs and let voice-mail take care of your telephone messages.

Teach your kids to focus on what is important instead of wasting time being busy with the little things that often have no relevance to their success in whatever endeavors they are involved with. Focus is one of the most critical contributors to success. Success can enhance self-esteem. Kids with healthy self-esteem are far less likely to become embroiled in senseless conflicts.

"Teach Time Management"

*Help your kids learn
that their greatest
amount of time should
be spent on their
most important goals.*

It has often been said that a goal not written down is not a goal. This same thinking can often be applied to helping your children identify their focus and organize their time.

Encourage your kids to write down all assignments, future tests, upcoming events, practices, etc., each day. Provide a specific book, or a place in an existing book, where these entries can be made according to day and date (the next section in this chapter will give you some hints on helping your kids organize and implement a plan to assist in completing each of these tasks). As your children complete their work, they will begin to understand the value of focusing on what is important instead of allowing themselves to be diverted by distractions.

PREVENTING CONFLICTS

2. PLAN EACH DAY BEFORE YOU BEGIN

Having spent a great deal of time coaching kids in various sports, I have often seen children who seem to be constantly looking for a parent who was unable, for one reason or another, to attend a game or practice. Many kids today are involved in a diverse spectrum of activities while many parents seem to be stretched to their limits with expectations at work along with the frustrations and unpredictability of daily traffic. These realities often cause family conflicts.

Some practical tips that can assist your family in avoiding the stress and conflicts that can be caused by too much to do in too little time are:

1. Place a large calendar in a prominent area of the house where all school and community events, activities, etc., are written down. This calendar should be checked by every family member at the beginning of each day (or the night before). If necessary, color code each family member.

2. Your kids should be encouraged to keep a wall calendar in their room where all school assignments, tests, practices, etc., are written down (this can also help you as a parent to be aware of what is happening in your child's life).

3. Teach your kids how to make a list of what has to be done each day. Things on the list should be prioritized with the most important tasks listed first. Help your kids understand that their most important tasks are the ones they should start with first.

As tasks are completed, your kids should put a bold stroke through the task on their list. Anything on the list that

"Teach Time Management"

remains undone for a few days should become number one, or should be taken completely off the list, the next time it is revised. It is not necessary to make a new list every day, although it is important to add any new items to it as they occur.

4. Before your kids start their homework, they should take their list from #3 above and set a tentative schedule regarding how much time will be spent on each task. This is one thing that could be checked by you each day. This helps to prevent your children from spending too much time on one task and failing to complete other things that have to be done. Schedules should also include times for regular breaks.

5. Mornings are often hectic times in many households leading to the possibility of stress and conflict before the day really gets started. By encouraging your kids to choose their clothes the night before, and by ensuring that all materials needed for school are set in a specific location, you can alleviate some of the possible problems. Families that wake ten or fifteen minutes earlier than they have to often enjoy a more relaxed start to their day.

6. For younger children (and perhaps even teenagers), maintain a specific convenient place in the house where they routinely put newsletters, announcements, etc., from school or from the teams and other organizations they belong to. This helps parents to be more informed without spending time looking for the appropriate material. The same location can be used for kids to pick up any notices that need to be returned to school after parents have signed them.

PREVENTING CONFLICTS

7. At the beginning of the school year, or semester, most schools send home a calendar of all events such as interview nights or reporting times for the year. Add all these events to your family calendar.

8. Car pool with other parents. A current problem for many parents is attempting to juggle the evening and weekend activity schedules for their children. Discuss with other parents the possibility of setting a schedule to take turns driving. It is a draining experience maintaining a full-time job and then spending your time off work as a taxi-driver. It is difficult to have quality time with your kids if you are worn out from a daily schedule that never gives you time for yourself. This problem is compounded when you have more than one child involved in different activities.

Less is generally more.

9. Transfer the schedule of your family activities and school related events to your daily planner at work. It is easy to forget a family activity when you are immersed in a busy day. An entry in your daily schedule can help to remind you of a game or a parents' night at your child's school.

10. Ensure that there is a specific convenient location in your house where all messages (telephone or otherwise) are kept.

3. LARGE TASKS ARE JUST A SERIES OF SMALL STEPS.

Many parents have experienced a child who leaves projects, assignments, and/or studying for tests until the last minute. Some kids in such instances will suddenly find themselves completely overwhelmed with what has to be done and as a result, either give up or do a poor job. In some cases, parents come to the rescue, especially in the area of projects and assignments, helping their child to complete what has to be done. Unfortunately, such help only reinforces a child's procrastination in completing tasks. If kids experience someone bailing them out at the last minute, they may grow up believing there is no need to plan ahead.

Encouraging your kids to plan ahead is not an easy task. Some parents would even go as far to say that it is impossible to teach kids how to take a large task and break it down into smaller steps to be completed a little at a time until the task is finished. One of the best examples to disprove such thinking relates to music lessons. There are many kids who master playing the piano, or some other instrument, by spending some time each day in practicing parts of a passage of music until the time comes when they have mastered the complete passage or technical exercise. The same is also true in sports and most other activities. Kids can, and do, master large tasks by working on a series of small steps over a period of time.

I am often amazed at the progress children make in

PREVENTING CONFLICTS

music lessons. I might add, from my experience with students, that there is often a very positive correlation between success in music lessons (or other structured activities) and success in school. Kids, who learn how to break down large tasks into small steps and who develop the discipline to work a little each day on completing these, are generally rewarded with significant achievements in their schoolwork. Once children experience the benefits of this approach to their work, it can develop into a lifelong positive habit.

> ***Whenever a job***
> ***seems to be too big,***
> ***help your kids***
> ***break it down***
> ***into manageable pieces.***

When your child has a major assignment or project due, help your child understand how the assignment can be divided into a series of steps. After identifying the steps, set a timeline for completing each one. As your child completes each part, he will feel some degree of satisfaction which can help motivate him to go on to the next step. The following case example shows how this approach can work.

Erik was assigned a novel of about 150 pages to read over a period of four weeks. In such situations, he normally procrastinated for as long as possible before he panicked. Erik was not a strong reader and such an assignment, when left to the last minute, became an impossible task for him.

In this situation, Erik's parents helped him to develop a schedule for reading the novel. The approach was simple. He would read 8 pages a day, five days a week, over the four weeks. By keeping to this schedule, Erik would actually complete the novel a day or two early.

Erik created a monthly calendar on his computer and typed in his goal of reaching page 8 on the first day, page 16 on the second, page 24 on the third, and so on. After he completed his 8 pages for the day, he put a bold stroke through his written goal with a bright highlighter.

Eight pages a day was manageable for Erik. He enjoyed stroking out his daily goal on his calendar. His calendar provided him with a visible reminder of his success. Soon 8 pages turned into 64. By completing a little each day, he learned to turn what would have normally been an insurmountable task for him into success.

In the process, Erik not only completed his novel, he learned a lifelong approach for completing difficult tasks.

PREVENTING CONFLICTS

4. NEVER MISPLACE SOMETHING TWICE

I remember reading a research study that concluded that adults, on the average, spent the equivalent of one year of their life, over their lifetime, looking for lost items. Whether this study was accurate, or not, the reality is that we all spend time and encounter stress as the result of looking for things we have misplaced. It might be our keys, a tool, a book, or a kitchen utensil, as examples. In some of these situations, as stress rises, the potential for a conflict within the family also mounts.

Most parents have experienced a child who has misplaced an assignment, a book, some clothes, etc. As the child searches for the lost item, tensions sometimes increase until a conflict occurs.

*If you find your kids
looking for the same thing
today that they
lost yesterday,
help them to organize in
such a way that they will
never lose
this object again.*

Wallets, keys, schoolbags, etc., all need a specific place to reside every day. When keys are stored in exactly the same place each day (and this location should be convenient to your entry into the house), this becomes a habit. Once this habit is formed, you will never waste time looking for your keys again. With your kids, it is useful to help them to develop similar habits. A small shelf, beside the door where they enter and leave the house each day, may be the perfect place for school related materials. After they complete their homework each night, the materials could be placed on this shelf ready for the next morning. Whenever they misplace an object, discuss possible methods to prevent this from occurring another time. Your kids may have other creative solutions. In the process, you are helping them to be better organized.

5. LISTENING IS TIME WELL INVESTED

The importance and power of listening is a theme that will be repeated throughout this book. As adults, we are often well aware of the time that can be wasted at work because miscommunication occurs. A customer complains, but nobody seems to have the time to listen. Suddenly, the customer takes his complaint to the company president, after which a great deal of time may be spent in resolving a problem that often becomes far greater than the original concern.

Similarly, miscommunication can lead to conflicts in the home. Effective listening, though, can make a positive difference.

Effective listening takes time. Failure to listen effectively generally ends up taking even more time. It takes less time to prevent a conflict before it occurs than after the fact.

> ***It takes less time
> to fix a problem
> before it happens.***

Although Chapter Five already presented some ideas on effective listening and the material on conflict resolution techniques in the second half of this book provides additional information, a few other considerations are:

TIPS FOR BETTER COMMUNICATIONS

1. Write your message on a piece of paper and hand it to your child as you state your message verbally.

"Teach Time Management"

2. As your child informs you of a request, write it on a piece of paper to take with you.

3. Ensure that your child writes your request into the appropriate date on his master calendar. If necessary, have him add it to his daily "TO DO" list.

4. Transfer your child's request to your daily calendar or daily "TO DO" list.

5. Repeat your child's request back to him to make certain that you understand what he has said.

6. Tell your child to repeat your message back to you to verify that he has understood you.

7. Avoid letting anyone else interrupt you when you are talking to each other.

8. Stop whatever else you are doing when you talk to each other.

9. Be specific in any things you ask your child to do. Where applicable, discuss timelines.

10. Give positive feedback to your child for taking action on your requests.

When things
are
going well,
take note
of what
you are doing.

CHAPTER EIGHT
Pay Attention To What Works

Sometimes, the most wonderful ways to prevent conflicts occur without even realizing it. For example, you are constantly struggling to get your child to do her homework. Then, one night you are sitting doing some work at the kitchen table when your child sits down beside you and begins to do her homework without any encouragement from you.

Sometimes, as in this example, you might find a solution to a problem without even realizing it. Maybe, your child finds some comfort in sitting beside you at the table. Perhaps, your child perceives you as doing some form of homework and is simply trying to copy you. The next night, you sit at the kitchen table and your child sits beside you again to do her homework. Over a few nights, by finding some work to do in the kitchen, you might help your child to develop a positive habit.

Many parents find themselves facing the same old problem with their kids over and over again. The conflict may relate to not doing homework, watching too much television, not getting enough sleep, etc. If you find yourself facing the same problem this week as you had last week, perhaps it is time to find a new approach for solving the problem. Generally, the same old ways for solving problems achieve the same old results. If you want a different result, it is important to change your approach to the problem.

Sometimes, a solution may appear when you least

PREVENTING CONFLICTS

expect it. The key is watching for those times when the problem seems to disappear. When this happens, ask yourself what you were doing at the moment it seemed to resolve itself.

> *Keep eliminating*
> *what doesn't work*
> *until you find*
> *what does.*

Jamie was a twelve year old boy who bullied others. There were often complaints from school and from other parents in the neighborhood concerning Jamie's aggressiveness with other children. His parents had tried various approaches to no avail.

One day, two children who lived next door, both who had been previous victims of Jamie's bullying, found themselves without a babysitter after school. Jamie saw the kids crying on their front porch. He approached them to discover that they were upset because their babysitter had not arrived and they didn't have a key for the house.

Jamie, accustomed to looking after himself following school, stayed with the children and helped them to settle down. Then he proceeded to play games with them.

When Jamie's mother arrived home, she found Jamie acting more responsible with the kids next door than she had ever witnessed before. The following day, she called Jamie's teacher and explained what had happened. His teacher arranged for him to assist in helping with younger children in the school.

Jamie flourished with his newfound sense of responsibility. His bullying others stopped.

A positive solution to a serious problem was discovered by accident.

Working
together
increases your
likelihood of
success.

CHAPTER NINE
Work Together

I am presented with many questions from parents as I conduct workshops. One of the most frequent and most emotional questions comes from parents who are in a situation where the child's other parent has a parenting style that confuses the child or even diminishes his/her self-esteem. While such questions often originate from single parents, this is not always the case. Some parents find themselves acting as a single parent even when their spouse or partner is still living in the same house. In this chapter, I will first consider a few general comments related to this dilemma and then offer some specific practical tips.

As the title of this chapter suggests, working together can help to prevent conflicts and encourage the healthy development of a child's self-esteem. A reality in most families is that parents do not always have exactly the same parenting style. Just as most kids adjust to a wide range of teaching and discipline approaches at school, they can also effectively deal with differing parent styles at home. It is helpful, though, for them when both parents support each other and attempt to communicate on issues that affect their children.

As parents ask me questions about their spouse, partner, ex-spouse or ex-partner, there is often an unstated question that reads something like, "How can I get my child's other parent to be more like me?" or stated in another way, "How can I get my child's other parent to stop undermining the positive things I am trying to do with our child?"

There are several possible responses to such questions.

First, if the other parent's approach is abusive to your child and endangers his/her safety, this is a matter that should be discussed with the police and appropriate health professionals in your community.

Second, it is important to continue to focus on what you are trying to do as a parent. The person you have the greatest control over is yourself. Being the best parent you can be is often far easier and more effective than trying to change the parenting style of another person.

*Give your kids
the best
of you.*

"Work Together"

Third, one of the most powerful ways you can affect what your child's other parent is doing is by demonstrating the power of effective parenting, of WINNING TOGETHER, yourself. If your parenting style is creating positive results, it is far more likely that other adults in your child's life will consider emulating your approach. By following the concepts and tips presented in this book, you can develop a WINNING TOGETHER style of parenting.

Fourth, you could suggest that you both attend a workshop together on parenting. Many communities offer such workshops as part of community health programs. Through these workshops, your child's other parent will be exposed to concepts and tips that originate from a neutral person, a person who is an expert in this area. This may help him or her to more readily consider the material offered.

Finally, it may be useful for you to realize that the parenting style you are opposed to may not be such a concern to your kids. Having worked for many years as a counselor with children, I am often amazed at how different teachers appeal to different kids.

I remember one morning when two very angry parents, let's call them Mr. and Mrs. Smith, demanded that their daughter be taken out of a teacher's class because, in their words, this teacher was an arrogant bully. This was an emotional conversation during which Mr. and Mrs. Smith presented a list of reasons why their daughter should be transferred to another teacher who was perceived to be a more approachable, fairer person. Less than an hour after this interview ended, I met two other parents, let's call them Mr. and Mrs. Jones, who presented their views on why they felt their daughter should be transferred into the class of the teacher who had just been berated by Mr. and Mrs. Smith. Kids respond individually to different parenting, or in this case, teaching styles.

Some parents find themselves as single parents. This might be the result of separation, divorce, illness, death, or in some cases is the result of another parent who is absent from the home due to work or recreational interests. Some tips for single parents are:

SUGGESTIONS FOR SINGLE PARENTS

1. When a parent is absent from a child for whatever reason, the child may want to talk about the absent parent. Allow your kids this possibility.

2. Single parenting does not have to be a curse or some stigma that you live with. Your attitude towards single parenting will shape your child's attitude. Strive to be positive and grow with the change.

3. Your kids should not be your messengers or your spies. Your most important focus with your children should be to let them just be kids.

"Work Together"

4.   You are still the boss. Your kids don't want to be equal partners or "little spouses". Be a parent first and a buddy second.

5.   Maintain firm, clear rules and boundaries. This structure can help your kids better deal with the other changes that are occurring.

6.   Allow your kids to enjoy being with their other parent. Kids need the love of both parents, even if they no longer live together.

7.   If one parent moves away, your children may worry about you leaving as well. In such cases, it is important to reassure them with your physical presence and your love. It is wise to avoid any expression of anger, in front of your kids, towards the parent who has left.

8.   Changes in financial well-being sometimes accompany single parenting. It is often necessary to move into another house or apartment, or even to another part of town. Attempt to maintain your child's routines as much as possible. Maintaining the same friends and attending the same school can be a tremendous help to them.

9.   Join a parent support group. As your kids see you attempting to deal in a positive way with the changes you are experiencing, they will be encouraged to grow as well instead of resisting the changes.

PREVENTING CONFLICTS

10. Single parenting often results in an overload of responsibilities. Strive to understand time management techniques and introduce them into your home.

11. Don't use single parenting as an excuse for either your current state of unhappiness or lack of success at work. Your kids will often model your reaction to the changes you are encountering. If you want them to grow up happy and successful, strive to be an example for them.

12. Regardless of how you feel about your child's other parent, don't use your child as your sounding board. Kids are kids and not mini-counselors. Children need to be able to feel that they can still love both parents. They don't need to know all the "dirt" you can throw their way.

13. Emphasize that parents are forever, regardless of where each parent lives.

14. Avoid directing your adult frustrations and concerns at your kids. Your children don't need to know about your dating concerns or your problems at work. Find adult friends or see a counselor to discuss these issues.

15. When children lose a parent, it is important to remember that every child grieves and reacts in his/her own way and with individual timelines. Patience is important for adults dealing with kids under such circumstances.

16. Resist spoiling your child with tangible gifts for no reason other than to make you feel better. Be a parent, not a briber.

"Work Together"

17.   Ensure that your child's other parent is informed of all matters related to his/her activities and progress at school. As uncomfortable as it might be, it is very beneficial for your child to realize that both parents are attending parent-teacher interview nights, etc.

18.   Kids tend to believe that most things in life revolve around them. This belief system makes it easy for children to blame themselves when divorce or even death occurs within a family. Reassure them that they did not cause whatever has resulted in you being a single parent.

19.   Spend quality time with your kids. Re-read the first chapter in this book titled, "Play With Your Kids."

20.   Be there for your kids. There is a natural tendency for some adults to overdevelop a new social life in reaction to losing a former partner or spouse. Your physical presence in the house can be reassuring to your kids. Strive for a balance between your needs and those of your children.

You are
what your kids
often
become.

CHAPTER TEN
Be A Friend To Yourself

We seem to be living at a time when most adults, and especially parents, seem to have little time for themselves. In fact, some parents even brag about how busy they are. Listening to some parents talk about their involvement in the lives of their kids, it becomes fairly obvious that some of these parents don't have a life of their own. Unfortunately, it is almost trendy to be overly busy.

It is difficult to be the best parent you can be when you are tired or even sick. It is difficult to be the best parent you can be when you are not feeling good about yourself or positive about your relationships with others. Sometimes, in order to help your kids, you may have to pay more attention to your own life. Some tips to help you to be a friend to yourself are:

1. TAKE SOME TIME FOR YOURSELF

It is an expected part of work that there are scheduled times for breaks, even if it's just lunch. It is equally important to take regular breaks in your role as a parent.

Spouses or partners can alternate taking a greater responsibility with their kids in order that the other person has a break for an evening or even for a weekend. Friends, relatives and neighbors can also be helpful. If one of your neighbors has similar aged kids, you might be able to arrange for each of you to have a break for an afternoon while the other person takes care of the kids.

When you establish a regular schedule for such

breaks, you know you will have some time each week for yourself. This can be a tremendous help to you in re-charging your own batteries and, as a result, help you to be more effective with your children.

2. PLAN AHEAD FOR POSSIBLE ILLNESSES

Your kids are going to get sick. This is a reality that every parent will face. In some instances, you may see symptoms of the illness before it takes your child out of school. Other times, the illness may strike out of no-where. When your child gets sick and is forced to stay home from school, this can present difficulties, especially if both parents work.

By planning for a possible illness before it happens, you can prevent stress and possible conflicts. Maybe, there is a neighbor, friend or relative who can help out. Perhaps, you can bank a few days from work for such a problem. Whatever the solution, you can prevent a poten-tial conflict by thinking it through beforehand.

The same may also be true of personal illnesses that either parent encounters. Staying home ill and looking after children at the same time is not an effective way to get better. Give some thought to possible arrangements that might be made in a situation where either parent be-comes ill.

It is also important to be proactive. Attempt to pre-vent illnesses in your family by emphasizing more sleep when your kids appear to be on the verge of getting sick.

3. EAT, SLEEP AND EXERCISE FOR WELL-BEING

Most parents have had experiences with their children when a child is overtired and hungry. In such instances, the normally best behaved child in the world can turn into the most difficult child. This problem can be even worse if he is also facing something new with his normal routines having been broken.

Although adults may not respond in the same exaggerated manner of a hungry, tired child, we do nevertheless suffer. Our behavior and effectiveness with others is negatively altered when we are tired and/or hungry. When you are not at your best, it is far easier to end up in conflict situations with your kids.

The path of least resistance often leads to more failures than successes.

It is difficult to pick up a popular magazine without seeing some article related to the importance of nutrition, sleep and/or exercise. Parenting can be an exhausting end to a long work day. Paying attention to your health needs can help you to be a more effective parent and help to prevent conflicts.

PREVENTING CONFLICTS

4. SPEND SOME TIME EACH DAY OUTDOORS

Some adults spend their entire day without ever being outside other than driving to and from work. A short walk, taking time to look at some flowers, trees or the sky can all lessen the stress that accumulates throughout the day.

Parents who take the opportunity to be outdoors with their children enjoy a double benefit: quality time with their kids and a healthier lifestyle for all.

Family conflicts are often caused by little things. A parent who is refreshed and feeling rejuvenated is far less likely to overreact to those little things.

5. UNDERSTAND HOW TO RELAX

Relaxation is a state of mind. As such, it can be practiced for short intervals throughout the day to alleviate stress. Meditation books and tapes can help to teach you how to relax. Evening courses in techniques such as yoga can also assist you.

Once you have learned how to relax, you can gain more from your walks or moments in the garden. You can enhance your breaks from work or from your kids.

A calm parent is better equipped to prevent conflicts than a parent who reacts aggressively or out of strong emotion.

A relaxed parent is also more effective in resolving problems in a WINNING TOGETHER manner when they do occur.

"Be A Friend To Yourself"

Further discussion on the importance of remaining calm in handling conflicts will be presented in the second half of this book.

6. SCHEDULE SOME TIME EACH DAY FOR YOURSELF

Most adults schedule their day in some way. Building five, ten, or even fifteen minutes for yourself into your daily schedule can help you to reduce stress. As you reduce stress in your life, you are more likely to avoid overreacting in conflict situations which generally causes them to escalate. Reducing stress in your life can also help you to go home at the end of the day feeling less tired and anxious. Your kids will benefit from a better you. It is far easier to avoid conflicts with your kids when you are not tired and stretched to your limit.

How you spend this time is your decision. The bottom line is that it is time just for you.

7. COMPLETE SOMETHING CONCRETE

Professionals, such as teachers, psychologists, social workers, etc., who work every day with kids, often understand the importance of having a hobby or interest that involves doing something concrete such as woodworking, gardening, a multitude of arts and craft possibilities, cooking, etc.

Sometimes, progress with kids can be slow and even go unnoticed. There are times when you may wonder if your kids are going to develop into responsible, happy and successful adults. In fact, there are times when many parents wonder if their kids are paying any attention at all to the things that they are telling them.

> ***Hobbies and interests can provide a sense of accomplishment and renew your energy.***

Effec-   tive parenting requires patience and a long term overview of how kids develop. Sometimes, it is difficult to maintain such a view. Having a concrete hobby allows you to see a finished result in something you are doing. Your success in your hobby can help you to be more patient with your kids. It can also help to remind you that success in any endeavor requires a plan that includes a series of sequential steps.

8. DO SOMETHING YOU LOVE AT LEAST ONCE A WEEK

What is one thing you love to do? Although this may have already been covered in the previous discussion in this chapter, it is possible the one thing that you love to do has been left unsaid so far. Your one love may be a hot, undisturbed bubble bath or listening to a special selection of music. It may be reading a novel or watching a movie. It may be writing in a journal or receiving a back massage. Whatever it is, find a way to do it.

Parents often go to great lengths to ensure their kids reach their activities, games and practices on time. Parents often spend a significant amount of money paying to help their kids participate in community and school activities and events. There are times when you need to be a little selfish. Attempt to pamper yourself each week with one thing that puts a smile on your face and makes you feel good.

9. AVOID PEOPLE WHO BRING YOU DOWN

It is easy to find people who love to talk about doom and gloom whether it's their family, the local news, world news, or simply their miserable luck. Avoid such people. Listening to their negative interpretation of living can depress you. When you are depressed, you are more likely to get into conflicts with your kids.

This does not mean that you ignore requests from other family members or friends who need you to listen to them, or need a shoulder to cry on. I'm referring to those people who continually moan and groan, intruding on your time and your happiness. Whenever you encounter such people, have an exit strategy. If necessary, you can suggest that they see an appropriate professional for assistance.

*One of the
greatest gifts
you can give
your kids
is
a positive attitude.*

10. BE A POSITIVE THINKER

Communication experts often remind us that much of what we say in our own minds each day is negative in nature. For most people, positive thinking is not a natural occurrence. Most people grow up hearing far more negative comments than positive. To be a positive thinker often requires constant monitoring of your thinking. When you catch yourself saying something negative, tell yourself to stop. Replace the negative thought with something positive.

The more you practice positive thinking, the greater the possibility will be for it to become a habit for you. This is one habit that is worth the time and effort.

It may help you to find books and articles written by positive thinkers. Read, and re-read the sections that inspire you.

A positive parent sets a wonderful role model for his/her children. Positive thinking can help to resolve conflicts in a WINNING TOGETHER way.

11. SPEND TIME WITH THE PEOPLE WHO BRING OUT THE BEST IN YOU

Do you know someone who really believes in you? Do you know someone who encourages you? Do you know someone who inspires you to be the best you can be? If so, these are the people you want to spend more time with. If you answered no, then these are the people you want to find.

Most parents realize the impact, either positively or negatively, that your child's friends have on them. Parents sometimes approach me asking how they can help a child who has fallen in with the wrong crowd. Adults can also be affected, either positively or negatively, by the crowd or individuals they spend time with. Try to spend your time with people who inspire you to be the kind of person you really want to be.

12. LAUGH

It has often been said that laughter is the best medicine. Whether it's another person, a book, a television show or perhaps even your children, spend time in situations where you can laugh.

PREVENTING CONFLICTS

Laughter reduces stress. A home where parents and kids are free to laugh provides an environment where conflicts have trouble growing.

13. LEARN TO FORGIVE YOURSELF

It is easy in the heat of the moment to say or do the wrong thing. Your reaction to your kids in conflict situations is the result of many factors. These factors include your love for your children in wanting them to become happy, responsible and successful people. Your reaction is also affected by your current level of stress which may relate to your day at work, your relationship with your spouse/partner, your financial situation, etc. Your reaction is also affected by the fact that there is no parenting manual that gives you the correct response for every situation.

When things don't go the way you would have liked them to, be willing to forgive yourself. You are human and as such, you are not perfect. Accept yourself instead of beating yourself up by saying things like, "I should have done this," or "I should have done that." Find peace within yourself first.

When you have forgiven yourself, then give some consideration to how you could better handle the same situation if it presents itself again.

In addition, you might want to talk to your child again letting him/her know that you feel things were not resolved in a winning way.

If it is appropriate, apologize. Your kids will respond

much better to you when they realize you are willing to admit when you have erred, although it is important to remember that this does not necessarily mean caving into their point of view. Forgiving yourself and establishing a new discussion with your child signals that you feel your previous method of handling the situation was inappropriate, but it does not necessarily mean your point of view has changed.

> **Sometimes, the most difficult person to forgive is yourself.**

14. CHECK YOUR STRESS LEVEL REGULARLY

We live in a rapidly changing world. For most people, change causes stress. We live in a world where job security for most people is a thing of the past, a world where violence seems to be increasing and a world where many people seem to be working longer hours. Each of these situations can cause stress. We also live in a world where kids are exposed to more misleading temptations than generations of the past encountered, once again causing stress.

Several ideas have been presented in this chapter to

help you alleviate some of the stress in your life. Unfortunately, you may not always be aware of your stress level. For those readers who generally feel a significant amount of stress, regardless of the reason, it might be useful for you to have your stress level assessed on a regular basis. For some people, your check might come simply from your spouse/partner or a friend. For others, it might be necessary to consult with a physician or a professional counselor.

Learning to recognize high stress levels in yourself can be a reminder to find ways to lower your stress before you attempt to resolve conflicts with your kids. When you are feeling stressed, small issues can turn into major conflicts.

Stress can be a normal by-product of the world we live in. Permitting stress to negatively influence you and your relationship with others, especially your children, does not have to be an acceptable choice.

Learn to identify what causes stress, and just as important learn what works best for you in reducing it.

15. HUG YOUR KIDS AT LEAST ONCE A DAY

Most parents realize that hugging their child is beneficial to the development of their child's self-esteem. Not as many adults realize the positive impact hugging can also have on parents.

As you give to your children, you will receive in return.

*Give your kids
random
acts
of
love.*

A hug is one of those wonderful moments when you tell someone else that you love them, and by reciprocating they give you the same message.

For parents who might respond that their kids avoid hugs or even react in a very negative way to your attempts to hug them, watch for the right moment. Even the most rebellious kids generally have lapses in character when you can grab a hug before they remember who they are trying to be. In extreme cases, give your kids a verbal hug without invading their physical space. Let them know that you love them without attaching any conditions to your love. In spite of their reaction, your kids will generally feel better, and so will you.

PREVENTING CONFLICTS

16. STOP COMPARING YOUR KIDS WITH OTHERS

There is a natural tendency for most people to compare what they have with what their neighbors or friends have. Comparing your children to others does not help you to be a better parent. Sometimes, other kids are not always what they appear to be. I have worked with young people who seemed to be models of success and happiness, yet when I got to know some of them better I sometimes found serious concerns underneath their masked exterior.

Let your kids be your kids. If you attempt to force them to be like someone else, you will often meet with a great deal of frustration and disappointment.

This is also true of siblings. When you compare your children with each other, you are likely to increase resentment, jealousy and competitiveness which will only serve to increase the number of conflicts in your home.

Look after yourself by parenting your kids according to the standards that are important to you.

17. IMITATE OTHER EFFECTIVE PARENTS

When you observe another parent effectively encouraging specific positive behavior from one of his/her children, don't hesitate to gain from the experience. Talk to such parents and learn from them. This is different than the example given above concerning comparing your kids to others. In this situation, you are trying to learn specific techniques in parenting that you see other parents using in productive ways with their children.

"Be A Friend To Yourself"

> *The fastest way to learn a new skill is by imitating another person who does it well.*

18. DON'T BLAME OTHERS FOR YOUR SITUATION

It is generally easier to blame others for our problems than it is to accept personal responsibility. Unfortunately, when we blame others, the problem(s) rarely go away. The best way to resolve a problem is by taking personal responsibility for finding a solution to it.

19. AFFIRM YOURSELF BEFORE GOING TO BED

The time just before you fall asleep can be valuable to you in looking after yourself. When you spend some of this time thinking about the things you did well during the day, you will not only enjoy a better sleep, you will feel better about yourself as well.

As you fall asleep, in addition to affirming the successes you enjoyed throughout the day, it might be helpful for you to consider your blessings as well. What are you thankful for? For some readers who face great difficulties with your children, this may not be easy. If you are able though to find some things to be thankful for, you will alleviate some of your stress.

> **Being thankful for what we have is healthier than being anxious about what we don't have.**

20. WORK ON YOUR SELF-DISCIPLINE

The number one person in your family that you have most control over is yourself. An important aspect of looking after yourself is keeping your focus on becoming the best you can be instead of spending most of your time trying to change others.

Your happiness comes from following your purpose. Self-discipline can provide you with habits that encourage success instead of just dreaming about what you want. The easiest way is not always the best way.

*Visualize
what you want
to accomplish and
then take action to
reach your goals.*

Self-discipline requires hard work, focus and commitment. The rewards can be great!

PART TWO

RESOLVING

CONFLICTS

The best solutions
occur when you teach your kids
how to successfully resolve conflicts.

RESOLVING CONFLICTS

INTRODUCTION

Conflicts are inevitable. The four steps presented in the following chapters can help you to resolve conflicts with your kids, when they occur, in a WINNING TOGETHER manner. When both sides in a conflict feel that the solution is in their best interests, there is a much greater chance the problem will be successfully resolved.

The four steps presented in PART TWO of WINNING TOGETHER can enhance the strategies and techniques you found in PART ONE of this book. In addition, there is a chapter that considers your current style of handling conflicts and the traits of a WINNING TOGETHER parent.

The final five chapters are:

11. BE A WINNING TOGETHER PARENT

12. REMAIN CALM

13. DEAL WITH THE EMOTIONS

14. FOCUS ON THE PROBLEM

15. FIND WINNING TOGETHER SOLUTIONS

Your basic
approach
to resolving
conflicts
can either
diffuse them
or
escalate them.

CHAPTER ELEVEN

Be A Winning Together Parent

This chapter considers two important factors that affect your success in handling conflicts:

1. What is your current conflict management style?

2. What are the traits of a WINNING TOGETHER style of parenting?

1. YOUR CURRENT CONFLICT MANAGEMENT STYLE

Read each of the following three paragraphs and select the one that best describes the way that you tend to handle conflicts with your kids.

PARAGRAPH 1

You tend to be a flexible person in your relationship with your kids. You generally present a calm exterior to your children, rarely yelling or shouting at them. You tend not to express what you are feeling or thinking inside to your kids because you don't want to hurt them. You are very good at accommodating the needs of your kids before your own needs. When you discipline your children, you are generally concerned about what they will think of you or whether you are being too strong on them. You tend to smooth over or ignore conflict situations. There are times when you say yes when you know inside you should have said no.

RESOLVING CONFLICTS

PARAGRAPH 2

You tend to be an inflexible person who has a very clear sense of right and wrong. You expect your kids to do what you tell them to and, if necessary, you don't hesitate to shout at them. You like to be in control of situations with your kids. You generally see yourself as the boss in your relationship with your children. You tend to be a strong disciplinarian. You tend to believe your kids should obey you and not question your requests or authority. You don't usually back away from conflicts. You generally handle conflict situations by telling your children what they should do.

PARAGRAPH 3

You tend to listen to what your kids have to say first before presenting your viewpoint. When you do speak, you are clear and direct in your expectations. You do not hesitate to tell your children what you are really thinking or feeling. You tend to act with confidence. In resolving conflict situations, you are willing to consider what your kids have to say. There are times when you will compromise your initial position in resolving a conflict. You rarely say yes when you want to say no. You don't ignore conflicts.

"Be A Winning Together Parent"

The preceding three paragraphs represent three conflict management styles. Which one best represents the way you generally handle conflicts with your children?

The three conflict styles corresponding to each paragraph are often identified as:

PARAGRAPH 1 - PASSIVE

PARAGRAPH 2 - AGGRESSIVE

PARAGRAPH 3 - ASSERTIVE

I have known parents with each of these three conflict management styles who were loving and effective parents. The following discussion isn't about whether you are a good or bad parent. It is an attempt to show you how your conflict management style can affect your attempts to resolve conflicts.

PASSIVE CONFLICT MANAGEMENT STYLE

Parents with this style of conflict management are often very good at smoothing over small conflicts. These parents tend to be very flexible and patient, two assets in handling conflicts successfully. Parents with a passive conflict management style also tend to be very considerate of their child's position or viewpoint which can be a positive factor in resolving conflicts.

The downside of a passive conflict management style is often a lack of firmness in stating your own viewpoint.

RESOLVING CONFLICTS

"No" often becomes "yes" which can create confusing standards for kids. Some children will eventually take advantage of a parent who lacks a firm approach. Passive conflict management parents tend not to openly discuss problems. This can result in conflicts continuing to escalate silently until some of them burst, or bury themselves deep enough that they cause physical and/or mental health problems. Some children who become passive themselves are easy targets for bullies and can be more easily dominated in relationships with others.

AGGRESSIVE CONFLICT MANAGEMENT STYLE

Parents with this style of conflict management can resolve conflicts quickly and to their satisfaction providing their children are accepting and/or passive in nature. An aggressive conflict management style of parenting can provide kids with a very clear sense of standards of right and wrong, as interpreted by the parent.

On the other hand, an aggressive conflict management style of parenting can fuel conflicts if children happen to be aggressive as well. Small conflicts can turn into major battles with neither side willing to back down or compromise. Some kids who comply with aggressive parents have a tendency to become bullies in an attempt to unleash the frustration and anger they are unable to express at home. Other kids may become passive because they are accustomed to being dominated by an aggressive parent. Such kids may become victims of bullying by their peers. When parents employ an aggressive conflict management style, conflicts can end with a potential winner (the parent) and a loser (the child). If children are constantly on the losing end, their confidence can suffer and low self-esteem can result.

ASSERTIVE CONFLICT MANAGEMENT STYLE

Parents with this style of conflict management can take some satisfaction that they are attempting to resolve conflicts in a manner many experts would support. Being assertive encourages open communications from both your children and yourself which can contribute to finding solutions for conflicts which are win-win in nature. Being assertive helps your kids to understand exactly how you feel. Kids benefit from honesty rather than being given cloaked messages.

Assertive parents are willing to compromise their position when presented with logical facts from their kids. This teaches your children that their opinions are valued and they are capable of contributing in a positive way to resolving disagreements.

In working with thousands of kids, I would suggest that there are relatively few problems with this conflict management style. One potential problem, though, can occur when assertive people attempt to always express their assertiveness. For example, some small conflicts with kids, especially those involving their siblings or peers, are sometimes best handled by ignoring them. This allows kids to learn to handle some of their own prob-

RESOLVING CONFLICTS

lems. In some of these situations, assertive parents may need to back off a little permitting their kids to develop skills in handling conflicts.

Another potential problem with assertiveness is the fine line that sometimes exists between being assertive and being aggressive. Confidence in stating your views and feelings accurately is important, but assertive parents need to sometimes ask themselves if their confidence is being interpreted by others as being aggressive.

2. TRAITS OF A WINNING TOGETHER STYLE OF PARENTING

I believe each of the three conflict management styles presented so far in this chapter have some positive attributes in successfully resolving conflicts with kids. In the following, I have identified seven traits of WINNING TOGETHER PARENTS. Some of these traits have their roots in the three conflict management styles that we just looked at.

When facing conflict situations, I believe WINNING TOGETHER parents are able to remain calm when facing conflict situations. In addition, WINNING TO-GETHER parents have the ability to know when to be firm and when to be flexible. WINNING TOGETHER parents are confident in their handling of conflict situations. They are skillful listeners and assertive in presenting their viewpoint. Finally, WINNING TOGETHER parents are able to work with their kids to find lasting solutions when conflicts do occur.

To summarize, WINNING TOGETHER parents are:

1. **CALM**

2. **FIRM WHEN REQUIRED**

3. **FLEXIBLE WHEN REQUIRED**

4. **CONFIDENT**

5. **SKILLFUL LISTENERS**

6. **ASSERTIVE**

7. **ABLE TO FIND WINNING TOGETHER SOLUTIONS**

The final four chapters in WINNING TOGETHER can help you as you strive to be a WINNING TO-GETHER parent.

Calmness
can be
contagious.

CHAPTER TWELVE

Remain Calm

People generally react in one of two ways to conflict by either fighting or fleeing. For most people, fighting is a verbal reaction which is often a defensive response, although it can also be an aggressive lashing out. For others, it may be physical.

The fleeing response is generally demonstrated by ignoring the conflict in some way. This might include changing the topic of conversation, attempting to lighten the seriousness of the situation, or even walking away as though nothing was happening.

While there may be some situations where you have no choice but to fight or flee, most conflicts are best resolved when you adapt a third approach that involves neither of these reactions. This approach requires you to stop your basic desire to fight or flee and instead remain calm. The first step in successfully resolving conflicts is to REMAIN CALM.

Remaining calm when someone else is verbally attacking can be very difficult for most people to do. (This book is not intended to provide instruction on how to respond if you are being physically attacked. For parents of kids who physically assault them, it is strongly recommended that you consult with both the police and appropriate medical professionals.) It is natural to want to respond. By reacting calmly, though, the likelihood is good that you may prevent the conflict from escalating.

RESOLVING CONFLICTS

*It is difficult
to fight
someone
who is calm.*

Some readers of this book may have children with concerns such as attention-deficit/hyperactivity disorder. In such instances, you are likely well aware that fighting fire with fire will dramatically increase the conflict. Remaining calm at the initial onset of a potential problem can greatly assist in keeping the conflict under control. Most other kids benefit from the same approach as well.

Let your kids say what they want while you refrain from reacting. You don't have to agree with what they are saying. It makes a lot more sense for you to present your views at a later time when they might actually be listening to you (there will be more on this in later chapters).

At the outset of a conflict, focus on remaining calm. Your calmness, even if you are biting your tongue with great effort, can work miracles in keeping the conflict from getting worse.

> Martha was a fifteen year old girl with a substance abuse problem. Having hid it from her parents for more than six months, the problem finally openly surfaced when she was caught with drugs at school. Her parents were called to meet with a vice-principal as part of the automatic suspension process for Martha.
>
> Martha knew her habit was out of control. For weeks, she had wanted to ask someone for help, but had resisted. As she sat in the vice-principal's office with her parents, she was embarrassed on one hand that her parents now knew about her problem, while on the other hand she was relieved because, with the support of her parents, she would now be able to receive some professional help.
>
> Once Martha and her parents were out of the school, her parents bombarded her with derogatory comments related to her character. She was a "tramp," "a whore," "a disappointment," "an embarrassment," and on the insults came with little connection to the actual substance problem Martha had developed.
>
> By the time they reached home, Martha was totally crushed by her their reaction. The moment the car stopped in the driveway, she fled. Within hours,

RESOLVING CONFLICTS

she had left the community.

It was more than six months later before Martha's parents established any further contact with her. By this time, Martha was working the streets. Her drug problem had increased.

More than another year passed before Martha agreed to participate in a drug treatment program as part of a conviction related to prostitution.

Eventually, Martha was reunited with her parents after they had all suffered greatly.

Perhaps, this story might have had a very different ending if Martha's parents had responded to her initial conflict with calmness. Perhaps, they would have heard her plea for help. Maybe, the problem could have been resolved allowing Martha to continue in high school. It is even possible that Martha and her parents might have grown stronger in their relationship instead of letting the conflict almost destroy them.

In my workshops on WINNING TOGETHER, I often use the acronym "WIN" to assist people in helping them to think of an easy way to remember the first step in successfully resolving conflicts.

W = WAIT

I = IMAGINE A POSITIVE OUTCOME

N = NEGOTIATE

"Remain Calm"

W = WAIT

Wait before responding to a conflict. In some cases, the wait may be a few seconds while in other situations you may decide to sleep on what has happened before you respond. The emphasis in waiting is on you achieving a state of calmness. Once your emotions come into play, there is a greater chance that you will get drawn into the conflict causing it to escalate. Calmness encourages rationale thinking which can be a tremendous benefit in resolving conflict situations. Calmness on your part can also decrease the emotional outburst on the part of your children.

It may be more beneficial for you to focus on your breathing instead of reacting.

I = IMAGINE A POSITIVE OUTCOME

There is a tendency for most people to increase their level of negative thinking in a conflict situation. If you are hoping for a positive solution, a WINNING TOGETHER resolution, it is important to erase any negative thinking from your mind and focus on possible positive solutions.

At the outset of a conflict, it may be too early for some parents to visualize a positive outcome. In such cases, you can visualize a happier moment between yourself and your child. Some people find it useful to briefly visualize a peaceful outdoor setting or a beautiful song. Whatever helps you to remove negative thoughts from your mind should be followed at such moments. As your

RESOLVING CONFLICTS

mind fills with positive thoughts, this will also help you to maintain a state of calmness.

N = NEGOTIATE

The word negotiate is a reminder that you are going to discuss the conflict in an attempt to find WINNING TOGETHER solutions instead of fighting it out or demanding your own way.

OTHER TIPS TO HELP YOU REMAIN CALM

Some additional tips that might be useful in helping you to remain calm in a conflict situation are:

1. ACCEPTANCE CAN CREATE CALMNESS

Some people move through life constantly struggling with conflicts that may be out of their control. Conflicts are a part of living. Accepting this fact may help you achieve a state of calmness. Instead of fighting against some problems that you may have no control over, you might accept the situation and then focus on how you can best live your life.

Parents, who have kids with problems such as substance abuse, legal issues, inappropriate peer groups, etc., may constantly fight such problems or even deny that they exist. Accepting the reality of a conflict can assist in finding personal calmness.

Sometimes, as parents, we have to resolve some issues in our own minds before we can reach out to help our kids.

2. LEARN HOW TO FEEL CALM

There are some people who don't know what being relaxed feels like. For such people, it can be very difficult to achieve a calm state when facing a conflict because their body and mind have rarely experienced this state before.

Whether it's through activities such as yoga, relaxation tapes, meditation workshops, or books, it is important to learn how to achieve a state of calmness. Once your body and mind are comfortable with this state, you can practice using these techniques to counter stress in your life.

The more proficient you are at relaxing, the easier it will be for you to remain calm when faced with a conflict situation with your kids.

3. FIND APPROPRIATE PHYSICAL RELEASES

It is a lot easier to remain calm with your kids when you regularly "dump" the stress of your daily life from your system. Exercise, that is appropriate to your health, can provide the vehicle to clean your mind and body of stress.

Conflicts are sometimes fueled by reasons totally unrelated to your children. A problem at work, a financial concern or a rebuff from a friend, can all increase the level of a conflict you are having with a child even though these events may be totally unrelated.

Give your best to your kids by cleansing your mind and body from undesirable stress.

4. FOCUS ON YOUR BREATHING

Deep breaths in through your nose and out through your mouth can help you achieve a state of calmness. As you breathe, focus on your breathing keeping negative thoughts out of your mind.

5. STRETCH

Whether it's through yoga, or exercises that you have learned as part of some other meditative or exercise program, stretching can help to release tension in your body. Stretching movements that make a difference for you have the advantage of being something you can often do even at work. A minute or two throughout the day can help you to maintain a relaxed feeling.

6. SMILE

Think of something that makes you smile or laugh. Smiling helps you to feel relaxed and remain calm.

7. SLEEP (or take an occasional nap)

We have become a sleep deprived society. If you know you are not getting enough sleep (and this is true for many parents), explore ways to better manage your day to allow you a greater amount of sleep.

8. LISTEN TO SOOTHING MUSIC

Enough said.

The focus of this chapter is on remaining calm when facing a conflict situation with your kids. Like so many other aspects of a WINNING TOGETHER approach to resolving conflicts, another huge advantage of remaining calm is that you are helping to teach your children how to respond to a conflict.

Once your kids learn to stay calm. or at the very least begin to mirror, even in a small way, your calmness, it will be a lot easier for you to successfully resolve problems without the anger, tears and destructive comments that often accompany family conflicts.

Many of the ideas presented in this chapter can also be used to help teach your children better anger management techniques. Teaching your kids to remain calm instead of lashing out at others can make a very positive difference in their initial attempt to control their anger.

Finding personal peace within can make a significant difference in finding peace with others. As you win personally, other people in your life can benefit from your success as well.

SUMMARIZING WINNING TOGETHER

STEP 1 - REMAIN CALM

Empathy
is the
great enemy
of
conflict.

CHAPTER THIRTEEN
Deal With The Emotions

Many conflicts present strong emotional responses. Sometimes, inappropriate things are said or done as a result of emotions overpowering logic.

The second step in successfully resolving conflicts is to DEAL WITH THE EMOTIONS.

Kendrick was an eight year old boy. He often expressed his disapproval through strong temper tantrums. His parents usually responded in turn by shouting at him to settle down. Most of the time, both sides continued to argue long after the initial cause of the conflict was forgotten.

Through counseling, both Kendrick and his parents agreed to try a different approach. When Kendrick's parents recognized Kendrick was about to lose control, or Kendrick himself realized he was about to explode, "time out" was called. The parents and Kendrick then went as calmly as possible to an area of the house that they had identified as their "quiet place." It was understood there could be no yelling or arguing in this location.

Both sides agreed to this arrangement providing:

a) Kendrick's parents remained calm and would listen to his concerns.

b) Kendrick would refrain from screaming and throwing objects.

The "time out" place allowed Kendrick to vent his emotions and concerns in more appropriate ways. His parents learned that they could avoid his temper

RESOLVING CONFLICTS

tantrums by remaining calm and permitting him to present his concerns without interrupting him.

Eventually, they all learned to work together at resolving issues without the need for having a time out place. As Kendrick mirrored the calmness of his parents, he learned better anger management skills and began to express himself in more appropriate ways.

Before conflicts can be successfully resolved, the underlying emotions should be addressed. Through effective listening skills, as outlined in both this chapter and the next, you can learn a few basic techniques that can make a significant difference in handling conflicts with your kids.

The following example of a conflict is presented two different ways. As you read the case studies, ask yourself which parental response seems to be the most effective in diffusing the emotions of the situation.

CASE STUDY 1

Sally, a thirteen-year-old girl, is having an argument with a parent concerning her homework.

SALLY: "I hate doing homework. I'd rather watch TV. Homework is a waste of my time."

PARENT: "I don't give a damn how you feel about it. Just get it done, or you won't be watching

"Deal With The Emotions"

TV again for a long, long time.

SALLY: "Go to hell. I'm not going to do it. You can't make me. I'll go live somewhere else if you try."

PARENT: "The hell you will. Go to your room right now and don't you ever talk to me again like that. And you're grounded for the next two weeks for talking back to me."

SALLY: "I hate you. You make me sick. One of these days I'm going to run away and then you'll be sorry."

CASE STUDY 2

Once again, Sally, a thirteen-year-old girl is having an argument with a parent concerning doing her homework.

SALLY: "I hate doing homework. I'd rather watch TV. Homework is a waste of my time."

PARENT: "Homework certainly seems like something you'd rather not do."

SALLY "You're right. Why should I give a damn about homework? It's just too hard for me anyway."

PARENT: "It's hard for you to do your homework when you don't understand it."

SALLY: "Absolutely. I'd rather just watch TV. At least that doesn't stress me out."

RESOLVING CONFLICTS

PARENT: "It would be easier for you to watch TV than to do your homework."

SALLY: "Yes. If I understood what I had to do, I wouldn't mind so much, but right now it seems like every teacher in the school is just out to get me."

In the two case studies presented above, which parent seems to be helping to diffuse the emotions? Hopefully, you chose the second example. In this example, the parent is using a listening skill known as paraphrasing. The parent is simply repeating back to Sally the intent of what she is saying. Paraphrasing helps to diffuse the emotions in a situation.

In the above examples, CASE STUDY 1 ends with both sides still arguing. The emotions are high. Instead of the conversation setting a framework for finding solutions to the conflict, the problem has escalated.

In CASE STUDY 2, Sally and her parent have reached the point where they are least talking. Instead of attacking her parent, Sally ends by blaming her teachers. Through the use of paraphrasing, the parent diffuses the emotions and establishes a level of communication where they can eventually discuss Sally's concerns about school and homework.

In conducting conflict resolution workshops for law enforcement officers, I have had seasoned veterans tell me that paraphrasing is a very effective technique for them. If police officers, who often face potentially violent situations, find paraphrasing an effective tool for diffusing conflicts, doesn't it make sense that parents will find this a useful skill to use as well?

Ten benefits you can gain by using paraphrasing when you are faced with conflict situations with your kids are:

BENEFITS OF PARAPHRASING

1. Paraphrasing give you an acceptable way to interrupt your kids. In most conflict situations, when you interrupt your kids, they will lash back at you and the problem grows worse. When you paraphrase, especially when you remain calm, you are simply repeating most of what they are already saying to you. This generally causes them to listen as they are really paying attention to what they have been saying.

2. Paraphrasing helps your children to calm down. Instead of fighting against you, they are listening. As you paraphrase calmly, you establish a softer level of conversation. Your kids will begin to respond to you in the tone of voice you use in paraphrasing.

3. Paraphrasing helps you to establish a conversation with your kids instead of an argument. Children will rarely fight back against a repetition of their own words. Their anger will begin to subside and you can eventually discuss their concerns in more appropriate ways.

4. Paraphrasing helps you to understand your child's point of view. Many kids often complain that their parents don't un-

derstand them. This perception often causes conflicts in the home. As you begin to understand your child's point of view, it will be easier to find WINNING TOGETHER solutions. Your kids will respect your efforts to understand what they are trying to say and, as a result, will be less likely to fight you.

5.   Paraphrasing can help your child to be more aware of what he is saying. As you repeat the essence of what is being said, he will be listening with great interest. There will be times when his mind is saying, "Did I really say that?" You will sometimes experience your child repeating something that he has said in a less drastic way after he hears you paraphrasing. As he begins to modify his position, you are already moving towards a positive solution, even though you have still not stated your point of view.

6.   Paraphrasing helps to create empathy. Simply stated, empathy is the ability to put yourself in another person's shoes. Empathy can diffuse conflicts. Empathy can help people understand each other and negotiate in a WINNING TOGETHER manner instead of fighting. When you empathize with what your kids are saying, you are genuinely attempting to put yourself in their shoes. By doing this, your children will be much more willing to work with you to find appropriate solutions.

7.   Paraphrasing can help to save face. Unfortunately, some conflicts occur in front of other people. One of the most difficult conflicts to resolve often occurs when you attempt to handle a conflict with your child when your child's friends and/or siblings are present. In such situations, your child may try to save face by standing up to you. Similarly, if your friends are present as you encounter a problem with your child, you may try to save face by overpowering him or her. In either

situation, paraphrasing gives you a "saving face" way out. Paraphrasing doesn't take sides or make demands. It does not embarrass or ridicule. By saving face, you can begin to handle the conflict without either of you feeling diminished in front of your peers, other family members or friends.

8. Paraphrasing helps to prevent you from stating your views and opinions. During the emotional first part of a conflict, your viewpoint, regardless of how logical it might be, may simply fuel the conflict resulting in a fight instead of finding a solution. Paraphrasing keeps you focused on what your child is saying. Your child does not have to argue against your demands or views. Once you sincerely understand your child's point of view, and the emotions have been diffused, you can then begin to present your views and opinions (there will be further discussion on this in Chapter Fourteen).

9. Paraphrasing helps to create respect. As you attempt to understand your kids, they will develop respect for the fact that you are taking the time to listen to them instead of demanding your way. The respect you establish by listening can pay dividends later when you present your viewpoint.

10. Paraphrasing is a skill that is invaluable for children to learn. As your kids learn to paraphrase, by the example you are setting, they will not only become better listeners when you speak, they will also become better listeners with other people. One of the number one skills employers are looking for in employees is the ability of a person to work well and communicate effectively with others. A major factor in maintaining positive relationships with others is the ability to listen. Paraphrasing can be the backbone of effective listening. As you paraphrase, you will be teaching your kids a skill that will be a tremendous asset to their future happiness and success.

RESOLVING CONFLICTS

Now that you understand a little more about the benefits that you can gain from paraphrasing, I would like to review the concept of paraphrasing again in order that you feel a little more comfortable with the skill.

As you paraphrase, you are attempting to capture the essence of what your kids are saying to you and repeating it back to them. It is critical that you do this without sarcasm or ridicule. Your voice needs to be calm and controlled. It is often useful to select key words that your child used when you are paraphrasing. Where strong emotions are involved, it is appropriate to identify the underlying emotions when you respond. For example, you might say, "You are feeling . . . when you . . . ." or "You are feeling . . . when I . . . ."

In some situations, you may find that after you paraphrase, your child immediately settles down allowing you to move on to Steps 3 + 4 of WINNING TO-GETHER (as outlined in Chapters 14 and 15). Other times, you may find yourself paraphrasing for a much longer period. The critical aspect of this step is that you avoid moving on to the next two steps until the emotions have been diffused. Finding WINNING TOGETHER solutions requires calmness and logical thinking from all the people involved in the conflict.

Similar to the learning of any other skill, your efforts to be a master listener need to be practiced with discipline. Instead of practicing with your children, I would suggest you find other opportunities to hone your skills. For most people, there will be many opportunities at work to use paraphrasing. You can also practice with your spouse/partner or friends. Where possible, work together with another person who can give you feedback on what you are doing. For those readers who would benefit from more structured help, many community colleges offer part-time evening courses in effective listening skills or conflict resolution techniques.

The following situations give you some additional examples of paraphrasing to help you better understand the concept.

SITUATION 1

> CHILD: "I don't have time to do my chores. I have to get my schoolwork done. I just have too much to do."

> PARENT (paraphrasing): "It sounds like you're feeling a little overwhelmed with everything you have to do."

SITUATION 2

> CHILD: "I hate my brother. He's always bothering me and losing my toys. I don't want to play with him any more. Keep him away from me."

> PARENT (paraphrasing): "Sometimes your brother can be annoying to you."

RESOLVING CONFLICTS

SITUATION 3

CHILD: "I'm not going to the store with you. I want to stay home. I always have to go to the store with you. It's boring."

PARENT (paraphrasing): "Sometimes going to the store with me is not the most exciting thing for you to do."

SITUATION 4

CHILD: "I don't want to go to bed now. I'm going to stay up and watch some more TV. I'll go to bed when I'm ready."

PARENT (paraphrasing): "You would like to stay up later and watch more TV."

CHILD: "Yes. I'm not ready for bed right now."

PARENT (paraphrasing): "You would like it if you could choose when you went to bed."

CHILD: "Yes, it's not fair that I can't decide. You get to go to bed whenever you want."

PARENT (paraphrasing): "It doesn't seem like a fair thing to you when I tell you it is time for bed."

CHILD: "Right. Why can't I just decide on my own?"

PARENT (paraphrasing): "You would feel better if

"Deal With The Emotions"

> there were times when you could make
> some decisions without me telling you what
> to do."
>
> CHILD: "Exactly, I want to be able to make some of
> my own decisions."

After reading each of the above examples, there may be some people who are saying to themselves, "Why not just tell the kids to do what has to be done and get it over with?" In most situations, I agree with you. Parents should be firm and direct with their children. Providing the requests are fair, most kids will do what you ask them to do. The important factor here is that we are not talking about most situations, we are looking at conflict situations. I am asking you to consider a different way of responding to your child if your normal way of handling things tends to result in heated arguments.

Similar to the above example, some children fight their parents night after night at bedtime. While I believe firm parents (those who teach their kids that no means no) will state their expectations and their kids will generally comply, there are occasions when some kids respond to firmness with great tenacity.

It is important to remember that kids need to exert their independence. This is a healthy part of growing up. In the above example (SITUATION 4), the paraphrasing could eventually lead to a positive discussion focusing on areas where the child might have a greater hand in making decisions (although going to bed whenever the child desires will not likely be one of them). The potential conflict can ultimately lead to finding ways for the child to become more responsible and more independent. These are benefits that might not occur if the child is simply ordered to go to bed on time night after night without considering her need to find appropriate ways to express her independence.

It is also useful to remember that this chapter focuses on diffusing emotions in a conflict situation. To this end, paraphrasing is a wonderful skill to employ.

Although there are two steps remaining in the WINNING TOGETHER conflict resolution process, there will be some conflict situations that resolve themselves by the end of steps 1 + 2. A calm approach, linked with skillful paraphrasing, often helps kids to achieve their underlying motive for engaging in a conflict: parental attention and understanding. Once they have achieved these, there will be many situations where the conflict is no longer an issue.

While some might argue that paraphrasing takes time, I would suggest that in the end it can save time. The goal of successful conflict resolution is to find solutions to problems that keep them from resurfacing. It is a lot less time-consuming to resolve a problem completely than have to continually readdress it every few days. Effective paraphrasing can be a positive step in helping to resolve many conflicts in a manner that prevents their reoccurrence.

"Deal With The Emotions"

Once you have established a calmer discussion with your child, you are ready to move on to the next two steps which are FOCUS ON THE PROBLEM and FIND WINNING TOGETHER SOLUTIONS.

<u>SUMMARIZING WINNING TOGETHER</u>

STEP 1 - REMAIN CALM

STEP 2 - DEAL WITH THE EMOTIONS

Don't let
your mind
make a
problem
bigger
than it
actually is.

CHAPTER FOURTEEN
Focus On The Problem

Once you have established an appropriate degree of conversation through your calm approach and paraphrasing skills, the next step is to focus on understanding the problem in its entirety.

> The night before a major project was due, Julie panicked. "It isn't fair that this was just assigned. There isn't enough time to complete it. What am I going to do?"
>
> Concerned about Julie's success at school, her parents assisted her in completing the project.
>
> A few weeks later, her parents were surprised when Julie told them that she received a failing mark on the assignment. In fact, she was so disappointed, she threw her work away.
>
> The next day, Julie's father telephoned her teacher for clarification. He was surprised to hear the following:
> - the project had been assigned seven weeks ago
> - Julie handed her project in a week late
> - she consistently wasted class time provided to work on the project
> - the project she handed in was only partially related to the topic that was assigned to her
> - the teacher had left voicemail messages for the parents with her concerns about Julie's lack of progress on the project

RESOLVING CONFLICTS

> It suddenly became apparent to the father that there were several problems related to this situation. His daughter had manipulated them into helping her complete the project. She had lied about when the project was assigned. She had wasted class time. It even appeared that she had managed to erase the teacher's messages from the family's voicemail to prevent her parents from knowing what was happening at school.

There are times, as parents, when we think we have a handle on a problem with our kids only to find it continuing to grow somewhat in the manner of Pinocchio's nose.

Identifying the complete problem is generally more important than trying to find a quick solution.

"Focus On The Problem"

Sometimes when parents are faced with problems, there is a tendency to ask their children, "Why?" Many times this question stops the conversation. The reality is that many kids don't always understand their behavior. As a result, it is generally best to avoid asking them this question.

Understanding a problem in its entirety requires the use of another listening skill, related to the way you ask questions, to assist in encouraging your kids to talk openly.

Questions can generally be divided into two types: open and closed. Closed questions such as, "How was your day?" or "Have you completed your homework?" generally result in one word answers. Closed questions can be useful to gather specific information such as, "Where does your friend live?" or "What is the date of your science test?" Closed questions, though, are not the best way to gather a wide range of information that is often necessary in understanding a problem. Responses to closed questions are usually too limiting to help you really understand your child's point of view.

Open questions are those that elicit responses that contain a greater degree of information. As a result, open questions can be very useful in understanding problems.

Open questions often begin with phrases such as:

Tell me more about . . .

Help me to understand . . .

Describe . . .

RESOLVING CONFLICTS

Give me another example . . .

Give me your point of view . . .

and so on . . .

The understanding of a problem is enhanced when your paraphrasing is followed with an open question.

For example:

> PARENT: "You are telling me that another boy in your class punched you for no reason?"

> CHILD: "Yes."

> PARENT: "Tell me what happened next." (or, "Tell me what was happening immediately before he punched you.")

Open questions are an excellent technique for stimulating conversation and attempting to understand what is being said. Open questions are often just open-ended statements. Open questions encourage your kids to talk about their concerns or their point of view in a conflict. This can help you to understand all aspects of the conflict from their perspective.

You can practice using open questions at work and with your friends. Combining the use of paraphrasing and open questions becomes a very powerful approach to help you successfully resolve conflicts with your kids.

"Focus On The Problem"

In addition to using open questions, there are a few other considerations that can be useful for you to think about in attempting to maintain your focus on the problem. These are:

1. **Deal with one problem at a time.**

2. **Learn to identify the smokescreens.**

3. **Clarify.**

4. **Summarize.**

1. DEAL WITH ONE PROBLEM AT A TIME

Your child is refusing to go to bed. In the process, your child swears at you. As you enter your child's room, you become aware that it is far messier than usual.

Instead of one problem, that of getting your child into bed on time, you are now faced with additional problems. If you attempt to deal with all these problems at once, you may lessen the possibility of finding solutions that are lasting. One goal of resolving conflicts in a WINNING TOGETHER way is to prevent the same conflicts from reoccurring time after time.

In this example, it is necessary for you to decide which problem is the number one priority for you to resolve. In some conflict situations with your kids, it is possible that there may be a long list of apparent problems. In such instances, it is useful to prioritize your concerns and begin with the problem that is highest on your list. There may be times when days or weeks go by before you reach the next concern on your list.

*Conflicts
are best resolved
one
at a time.*

2. LEARN TO IDENTIFY THE SMOKESCREENS

Most kids go through a stage of responding to parental requests with some form of temper tantrum. While this may be a normal part of the development of a three-year-old, it is no longer appropriate for a ten-year-old. Older children may continue to exhibit temper tantrums because they help them get what they want, or in some cases avoid what they don't want (which may have been some form of discipline).

For some kids, temper tantrums, crying, joking, swearing and other forms of inappropriate behavior are sometimes just smokescreens. While smokescreens, in themselves, may be a problem, you need to be careful that they don't divert you from the initial problem you were trying to resolve.

When you encounter these diversionary responses from your kids, it is important to remain calm, paraphrase if necessary, and let the reaction (usually in the form of an inappropriate emotional response) evaporate. Once this happens, focus again on the problem at hand. Let your child know that you are going to return to the problem that was being dealt with. Sometimes, one of the best ways to stop your kids from having temper tantrums is to ensure your initial concern that they were trying to avoid, by expressing their temper, continues to be your focus until it is resolved. Once your children learn that their temper tantrums can't distract you, their outbursts often cease.

An unwavering focus is a prerequisite for success.

3. CLARIFY

As your kids are talking to you, it is important for you to clarify what they are saying to help you understand them. While paraphrasing and the use of open questions can help you immensely in understanding the problem, it is also useful to ask your children to clarify what they are saying to you.

The following situation provides an example of clarifying what a child is saying.

PARENT
> "So, you're telling me that when try you to share a toy with Billie, he screams?"

CHILD
> "Not exactly. He takes my toys from me when I'm playing with them."

PARENT
> "So you're playing by yourself and he just comes along and grabs one of your toys?"

CHILD
> "Sort of."

PARENT
> "Sort of? Tell me what you mean by sort of."

In this situation, the parent is using paraphrasing and open questions in an attempt to clarify what her child is saying. Similar to the previous discussion on ignoring

smokescreens, it is important to maintain your focus. Let your child know that you really want to understand what he is telling you. By clarifying what he is saying, there is a much better chance you will understand the problem at hand, at least in his eyes.

If your kids are vague in what they say, ask for specific examples. Be persistent until you know exactly what they are talking about. The following situation provides a sample dialogue where a parent asks for specific examples to help clarify what is being said.

CHILD
"Everyone is picking on me at school."

PARENT
"Picking on you? What do you mean by this?"

CHILD
"The other kids are always hitting me and saying bad things to me."

PARENT
"That must be very upsetting to you. Give me some examples of when this has happened."

CHILD (pausing)
"Yesterday, one of the girls in my class said I was stupid."

PARENT
"She said something unkind to you. Tell me about some other times when kids were hitting you or

saying some unkind things to you."

CHILD (pausing)
"I don't really remember. I just don't like it when the other kids pick on me."

PARENT
"It is upsetting to you when kids pick on you. Tell me about some other times when this has happened."

CHILD (pausing)
"Well, last year another boy and I bumped into each other at recess. He told me I should be more careful where I was going."

PARENT
"You both bumped into each other. What are some more examples?"

CHILD
"I don't really remember any. I just didn't like it when Jennifer told me I was stupid."

Without prolonging this example, I think you can begin to see how the parent is attempting to clarify a possible conflict situation. By asking for specific examples, the parent can ascertain the extent of the actual problem. In the case of possible bullying, though, I would not let the conversation drop just because the child became evasive. Sometimes, kids are too embarrassed to provide all the details of what is happening. Clarifying may also require you to talk to someone else, such as a teacher, a sibling, or a friend in order for you to understand what your child is really attempting to say.

*Verify
the problem
before you
seek
a solution.*

4. SUMMARIZE

Once you think that you have a fairly good grasp of the problem, summarize everything that has been said. Summarizing is similar to paraphrasing except that you may be taking a greater amount of material and restating it as concisely as possible.

After you summarize, if your child responds with words or phrases such as, "Yes," "That's it," or "Exactly," you know you are ready to move on to the final step of WINNING TOGETHER.

If your child responds with words or phrases such as "No," "That's not what I'm trying to say," or "I don't agree with everything you're saying," then it is necessary to go back a step and clarify once again. To make things a little easier when this occurs, it is useful to ask your child what she agrees with and what she disagrees with. If necessary, repeat your summarization a sentence at a time providing an opportunity for your child to clarify herself after each sentence.

Once you are able to summarize what your child has told you with no objections, you are in a position to move on.

In situations involving more than one child, it may be necessary to clarify and summarize what each child is telling you. Although this is obviously time-consuming, it will be well worth your effort in the end if you are able to resolve the conflict in such a way that the problem never occurs again. A bonus in taking the time to repeat these steps with each child involved is that your kids are learning skills in successfully resolving conflicts.

When your children walk through the steps involved in WINNING TOGETHER, the real reward will be seeing your kids begin to use the process to solve their own conflicts. When this occurs, you will have the satisfaction of having taken potentially stressful situations and turned them into opportunities to help your kids to develop into responsible and successful people. The ability to effectively resolve conflicts is a skill that is a tremendous asset to anyone throughout his or her life.

When you focus on a problem until you really understand it, you are also helping your child to understand it better as well. There will be situations by the end of this step, in WINNING TOGETHER, when your kids will simply shrug and say, "Now I know what I have to do."

"Focus On The Problem"

Solutions are much easier to find when a problem is completely understood.

Get all the facts before you decide what the problem really is.

SUMMARIZING WINNING TOGETHER

STEP 1 - REMAIN CALM

STEP 2 - DEAL WITH THE EMOTIONS

STEP 3 - FOCUS ON THE PROBLEM

Sometimes,
in order
to do things
differently,
you need
a new set
of tools.

CHAPTER FIFTEEN

Find WINNING TOGETHER Solutions

The phrase WINNING TOGETHER implies three things.

First, in attempting to resolve conflicts, the word "WINNING" suggests that you strive to find solutions where both you and your child win. These solutions, as much as possible, save the face of all involved. The solutions are neither embarrassing nor humiliating to anyone. They are solutions that everyone feels are the best possible choices to resolve the conflict.

Second, the word "TOGETHER" suggests that these solutions are a cooperative effort. When both you and your child contribute to finding a solution, it is generally easier for both sides to feel good about the final result. When you work together, it is easier to find win-win solutions. Solutions, that involve the input of both you and your child, are generally solutions that work. A good solution not only resolves a conflict, but helps to prevent it from reoccurring. You are winners together.

Third, WINNING TOGETHER provides a process for effective conflict resolution. As you and your child engage in this process, you are not only resolving the conflict at hand, you are also teaching your child lifelong skills in conflict resolution. These skills can be invaluable to the future happiness and success of your child. When this occurs, you win by having the parental satisfaction of having contributed in such a positive manner to the future development of your child. Your child benefits by learning a set of skills to assist him/her in facing the conflicts that will come his/her way as part of life. You both win together.

Before I outline six methods for achieving WINNING TOGETHER solutions, I would like to offer ten thoughts that may be useful for you to consider before working with your child to find lasting solutions.

THOUGHTS TO CONSIDER
IN RESOLVING CONFLICTS

1. If you have faced this same problem on numerous occasions in the past, it is likely time to look for a solution that is different than those that you used before.

2. Don't let yesterday use up too much of today. The past is the past. Learn from it, but don't dwell on it. Let today be a fresh start.

3. When you are facing a huge problem, look for some small part of it that you and your child can reach agreement on.

4. You don't always have to see immediate results for progress to be occurring.

5. Visualize a solution that is good for everyone involved. It is difficult to achieve something that you can't see.

6. Most solutions come dressed in work clothes. Hard work and commitment now can pay dividends later.

7. Sometimes, when you take a step away from the problem, it begins to look a little different.

8. The major limits on solving problems are often those that your mind sets.

9. If you can't solve a problem, learn how to manage it.

10. Mastering one problem effectively is usually more valuable than handling many problems poorly.

The following are six possible methods for achieving WINNING TOGETHER solutions:

1. Ask your kids what they think is fair.

2. Provide choices.

3. Take the best of the possible solutions.

4. You decide.

5. Seek help from a third party.

6. Learn to manage the problem.

RESOLVING CONFLICTS

1. ASK YOUR KIDS WHAT THEY THINK IS FAIR

By the time you have completed steps 1-3 of the WINNING TOGETHER process, there is a

> *Unless you have*
> *a better way*
> *of doing it,*
> *don't criticize the suggestions*
> *you have been given.*

strong likelihood that your child may have some excellent ideas on solutions to the conflict being discussed.

For example, a problem exists with your child related to watching too much television and completing too little homework. This has been an ongoing problem. You have tried everything you can think of related to resolving the problem to the point of disconnecting the television. Every time you attempt to resolve this issue, your child becomes angry and sometimes even hostile. You have been called "unfair," "uncaring," "mean," and other names much worse.

Tired of the endless fighting concerning this issue, you try a different approach. During a relatively quiet time, you calmly tell your child you would like to find a solution to this problem and would appreciate her help.

Using your best paraphrasing skills and open questions, you seek to understand your child's point of view. During this moment of calmness and understanding, your child states that she would like to do better at school. You resist stating your viewpoint and continue to focus on what your child is saying. Eventually, you ask her if she can think of any solutions.

Your child states something to the effect that maybe she could do her homework first before watching television. Once again, you resist reminding her that you tried to enforce this suggestion weeks ago. You agree this might be a good idea, but you ask, "How will I know when your homework has been finished?" Your child replies, "I will show you a list of what has to be done each night. When I finish my homework, you can check it off on the list."

While this example may sound like it is too good to be true, I have seen this approach work with many kids. When parents take the time to listen to their child's concerns in a calm manner, WINNING TOGETHER solutions are often reached. In the above example, both the parent and the child were able to accept a solution which pleased both of them. The solution had the added benefit of being suggested by the child which made it easier to enforce when the child needed a gentle reminder of "her" solution.

In many conflict situations, you will have a good idea of your child's position after you complete steps 1-3 of WINNING TOGETHER. If her position is close to

RESOLVING CONFLICTS

yours, ask her for potential solutions. There is a very good chance, in these situations, that you will reach WINNING TOGETHER solutions fairly easily.

Even when you are uncertain of your child's position, it is useful to ask her for possible solutions. This helps you to understand what is fair for her. This may assist you if you need to move on to any of the other strategies presented in this chapter.

Finally, by asking your kids to suggest solutions, you are telling your children that you value their opinions. Your kids learn that you are hoping for a cooperative effort in resolving the conflict. Children often show a much greater degree of responsibility when they are given more responsibility.

Sarah and her parents were locked in a battle concerning her curfew on weekends. Her curfew was midnight. She had repeatedly broken this curfew in the past few months in spite of grounding and having other privileges taken away from her. Sarah wanted to stay out later than midnight. Her parents refused to compromise their position.

Sarah threatened she would run away. Her parents threatened she would never be allowed out of the house again. The battle raged affecting everyone in the family and Sarah's schoolwork.

One week night, when things were calm in the household, Sarah's parents suggested that they talk about the problem, making it a point to request

Sarah's help to find a solution that was agreeable to each of them. Sarah presented her views which her parents listened to carefully using paraphrasing and open questions to seek understanding. Sarah's major request focused on being able to watch videos at the homes of various friends in situations where their parents were home. Sarah's parents were eventually able to present their concerns related to safety issues.

Once both sides had calmly presented their views, Sarah's parents asked her if she could suggest any solutions. Sarah suggested that her curfew remain at midnight unless she discussed beforehand her need to stay out later. In such situations, she would provide the telephone number of where she would be. In addition, her parents could verify there would be parents at this house. Sarah also agreed her parents could pick her up from the house at a time which they mutually agreed on.

Sarah's suggestions, with a little fine tuning, became the basis for a WINNING TOGETHER solution. The solution ended the fighting and set a framework that addressed the concerns of everyone involved. The solution also gave a degree of greater responsibility to Sarah, a positive factor in the development of her own self-esteem. The process leading to the solution also established a framework that they could use to resolve any future conflicts in a WINNING TOGETHER manner.

Asking your kids for input to suggest possible solutions can be a very effective way to achieve WINNING TOGETHER results.

RESOLVING CONFLICTS

2. PROVIDE CHOICES

Sometimes, WINNING TOGETHER solutions come as the result of offering choices to your child. A three year old is resisting wearing a T-shirt that you have selected. As your efforts become stronger, your child's refusal becomes greater. You try to force the T-shirt on to no avail. Your child is now screaming. You are frustrated and angry that such an apparently simple task could have grown into such a stressful situation.

Another parent faced with the same problem has learned from past experience that inflexibility leads to major conflicts. This parent offers her child choices. Two or three T-shirts are selected by the parent. The child chooses from these options. The parent wins by having the child wear something that is appropriate. The child wins by being able to express her independence in making a choice.

Finding a way
that is less rigid
just might be the answer
for resolving a conflict.

There may be occasions when you present several choices to your child in an attempt to resolve a conflict and he refuses all your choices. The following provides some additional thoughts on how to respond to such situations.

In offering choices, your child is going to be more agreeable if you understand his point of view and have kept this in mind when making your suggestions. When nothing seems to be working, don't hesitate to ask your kids if they have other choices you might add to your offering.

When your child simply refuses to cooperate in selecting a choice, even after you ask for his input into possible additional choices, it may be necessary to say, "Either select one of the options I have given you, or you will be choosing for me to make the choice for you." By continuing to tell your child that he is making the choice, you are diffusing some of the potential anger that might result when you have to enforce the decision to be made.

Ricardo was often involved in bullying other kids both at school and in the neighborhood. There were few kids in Ricardo's life who hadn't been a victim at one time or another of his taunting.

Through counseling, Ricardo began to understand the importance of stopping his hostile

RESOLVING CONFLICTS

behavior. Unfortunately, though, he still had difficulties controlling his behavior. Ricardo just didn't seem to know how to respond to most other kids in an acceptable manner.

With a counselor's help, Ricardo learned some other choices. He learned he could keep quiet and not say anything at all. Another option was to find something complimentary to say about the other person. Another option was to talk about school or even the weather.

In a controlled situation, Ricardo learned to choose one of the options, he had been taught, when he encountered other kids he had once bullied. Soon, he was replacing his bullying behavior with more appropriate conversations at school and in the community.

By realizing he was making the choice in each situation, he was able to feel that he was in control. This helped him to express his independence in a far more positive manner than bullying.

3. TAKE THE BEST OF THE POSSIBLE SOLUTIONS

Some conflict situations are not easily solved. Your conversation with your child seems to go on and on with little progress being made. In such situations, it may be helpful to employ a process which takes the best ideas you have each suggested and develop a WINNING TO-GETHER solution from them.

For example, two children regularly fight over computer time in the home.

Over the course of the conversation, both kids have suggested some possible solutions. The solutions include:

- buy another computer
- use the computer on alternate evenings
- set a schedule each evening
- go to a friend's house where there are
  several computers
- take turns going to a library each evening to work
  on a computer there

Underlying this list of suggested solutions are two concerns that need to be kept in mind in finding a WIN-NING TOGETHER solution. The first concern is that the oldest child has more homework and a greater need to use the computer. The second concern is that both kids have a tendency (which often causes conflicts) to play games on the computer instead of doing homework.

The parent eliminates buying another computer and going to a friend's house from the list. While setting a schedule each day seems to be the best solution, the parent is concerned about the possible time involved in setting up this schedule to be agreeable for both kids.

In the end, the boys agreed to an arrangement where they would alternate usage of the computer an hour after school each day for the purpose of playing games. After dinner, the youngest child was given use of the computer for one hour to do his homework. When his homework was finished, he was not permitted to play games during his allotted homework time. The older child was given the next two hours each evening to do his homework and once again, he could not play games during this time. The boys agreed that during the remainder of the evening, and on weekends, they would set their own schedule for usage. If necessary, a parent would mediate any conflicts that arose from scheduling these additional times, but the boys would each lose one hour of after school computer playing time for every occasion one of their parents had to mediate further computer related conflicts.

By selecting the best components of possible solutions, and by understanding the needs of each child, the parent and kids were able to cooperatively find a creative solution to their problem. Each person was satisfied with the solution and the identified procedure for resolving future conflicts. In addition, the boys learned some skills in conflict resolution and a motive for using these skills when future conflicts over computer time arose.

4. YOU DECIDE

You have listened to your child's point of view. You have worked hard to understand your child. You have even asked for possible solutions and, where possible, attempted to work cooperatively to find solutions that were in everyone's best interest. Unfortunately, you have not been able to agree on a solution that is best for everyone.

In such a situation, if you feel agreement is close, I would suggest you all sleep on it for a night and take another crack at it tomorrow.

If agreement is still light years away, I believe that it is in your role as a parent to make the best decision based on all the available information. There are times in a business when the boss has to end the discussions and make a final decision. Similarly, I believe that there are times in the home when a parent has to take charge in the fairest possible manner.

In such situations, both the process and the solutions can still be a WINNING TOGETHER experience. Your child has learned more about conflict resolution as a result of the process. She has also learned the reality that, in the end, someone else may make a decision for her if a cooperative agreement in not reached. Your resolution can still be a WINNING TOGETHER solution if you consider the needs of everyone involved when you make your decision.

> Kari wanted unrestricted telephone privileges in the home. If she wasn't permitted to use the telephone whenever she wanted, she would purchase her own telephone.
>
> Her parents were concerned about the inappropriate amount of time Kari spent each evening talking on the telephone at the expense of her homework and relationship with other family

RESOLVING CONFLICTS

members.

This conflict had been ongoing for months with both sides expressing anger and frustration. Discussing the problem with Kari resulted in no solutions. Kari was determined to do what she wanted in spite of her parent's concerns. Through the discussions, her parents became more aware of her needs. One need was simply for socializing with her friends. Another need related to discussing her homework assignments with friends. Another need related to the problem of a television blaring in another room in the house when she tried to do her homework. Her parents had observed that on most nights Kari had approximately two hours of homework.

Her parents decided to implement the following solution. Kari was permitted one hour each school night to talk on the telephone (if she decided to purchase her own telephone this one hour limit would still apply). During the two hours immediately after dinner, all televisions in the house would be turned off helping Kari to concentrate on her schoolwork. When Kari encountered any difficulties with her schoolwork, she would ask her parents for help. If they were unable to help her, they would give Kari a specific length of time to telephone a friend for assistance. It would be Kari's responsibility to inform her friends when she would be available for telephone calls. As weekend telephone usage had not presented a problem, no restrictions were placed on this time.

> Although Kari initially reacted strongly against this unilateral decision, within a week she was accepting it. It didn't take much longer for her to realize her schoolwork was benefiting from the solution, not to mention an improved relationship with her parents. She enjoyed the opportunity to spend more quality moments with them each evening. Over time, the decision became a WINNING TOGETHER solution.

In the above example, Kari realized fairly quickly that the decision made by her parents was a fair one that was in her best interest. This is certainly not always the case. There will be situations for most parents when they must make an unpopular judgment that their kids rebel against. There may be occasions when some children take years to realize the benefits to them of resolutions imposed by their parents. In some cases, kids may never understand the impact of a decision made years before even though the results of it may still have helped them.

A key in implementing decisions made by you is to be both firm and calm. In addition, the results will be more effective when you have taken the time to truly understand the conflict from your child's point of view.

I believe these are still WINNING TOGETHER solutions even though your kids may not be aware of the immediate benefits to them.

RESOLVING CONFLICTS

5. SEEK HELP FROM A THIRD PARTY

There may be times when you and your kids find yourselves in a conflict situation that you are both too emotionally involved in to find a solution that is in everyone's best interest. On other occasions, you may find that you are very close to achieving a WINNING TOGETHER solution, but you just can't agree on one or two small issues. In such instances, it might be helpful to have another person listen to both sides of the problem to help you reach your final solution.

Ideally, this person should have some familiarity with conflict resolution techniques, as well as being a person who can remain objective. Both parents and kids need to view this person as fair.

When you involve another person to help, you might decide that this person will guide you towards a final decision, or you might decide that this person actually has the authority to make the final decision. In either case, these ground rules should be established before the person is consulted.

The more serious the conflict, as determined by both yourself and your child, the greater the need will be to employ a professionally trained mediator to resolve your outstanding issues.

Your child's teacher, school social worker and/or family doctor may be able to assist you in selecting an appropriate professional to assist in mediating the conflict.

6. LEARN TO MANAGE THE PROBLEM

You have tried the ideas presented in this book (including seeking professional help) and serious problems still remain with your child. In some cases, the conflicts may be the result of physical, intellectual or psychological concerns that cannot be treated easily. In some instances, they may never be resolved. In these situations, when all else fails it may be necessary to learn to live with the problem. In such situations, I recommend that you seek professionals who can assist you in finding both peace and balance in your life.

A family faces a conflict because a parent has cancer. While there are elements of this problem that can be discussed and resolved (such as everyone taking greater responsibilities in the home to alleviate the tasks this parent once had), it is possible that the illness may reach a point where there is no immediate, or long-term, solution. In this situation, when family members are able to accept the conflict by managing it instead of trying to resolve it, there is the potential for more harmony within the home, even though the major source of conflict has been left unresolved.

A single parent struggles with a teenager who refuses to go to school. The tips and strategies within this book, as well as others, have all been tried to no avail. Worn out from trying to resolve this problem, the parent finally decides to accept it and learn to manage it. The problem is left with the teenager as the parent attempts to move on with living. Although the problem has not been resolved,

RESOLVING CONFLICTS

the parent is able to find a sense of personal peace knowing that every avenue related to the problem has been explored.

Sometimes, it is necessary to accept the reality that some conflicts cannot be resolved, at least not in the present moment. In these situations, parents need, as difficult as it may be, to let go of the problem. Sometimes, kids have to face the consequences of their own decisions before they may be willing to admit that they have a problem.

By letting go of the problem, parents can refocus on achieving their own well-being and reach out to other family members who might have been ignored during the struggle to resolve the conflict with another child.

As stated earlier, I believe it is important to seek professionals in the community who can assist you when you face such a circumstance.

SUMMARIZING WINNING TOGETHER

STEP 1 - REMAIN CALM

STEP 2 - DEAL WITH THE EMOTIONS

STEP 3 - FOCUS ON THE PROBLEM

STEP 4 - FIND WINNING TOGETHER SOLUTIONS

SOME FINAL THOUGHTS

Now that you have finished reading WINNING TO-GETHER, I would suggest, as I did at the beginning of this book, that you select one idea that you feel could make a difference, however small, in your home. Introduce this idea calmly and with purpose. It is best not to try to make too many changes with your children too quickly. Kids like routines, even if the routines are contributing to the problems.

As you find success, begin to implement other ideas. Your kids may have taken years to learn their current state of behavior. To effectively resolve some conflicts may require both patience and perseverance.

Achieving WINNING TOGETHER results can require both dedication and focus. The benefits your children receive from learning the process can be positive and lifelong.

It is also recommended that you seek other books, workshops, and other sources of information related to this topic. No single book can provide answers unique to every conflict. Being an effective parent often requires a concerted attempt to regularly learn new approaches and validate the skills you already have.

The way you resolve conflicts with your kids can truly make a difference in helping them to develop into happy, responsible and successful adults.

ABOUT THE AUTHOR

Brian Harris has extensive experience as a counselor and educator. He has worked in elementary and secondary schools, as well as community colleges. For more than fifteen years, he taught counseling courses part-time through the University of Toronto and York University to professionals who work with kids.

Brian also worked ten years as a counselor on a Tragic Events Response Team.

He has presented workshops on WINNING TOGETHER to police officers, probation workers, social workers, counselors, teachers, school administrators, parents, and staff from various companies. Audiences appreciate his practical proven tips in helping to resolve conflicts and his entertaining presentation style. He is the author of eleven books with sales of more than 300,000 copies. You can find additional information on Brian's presentations at:

www.winningtogether.ca